A Student's Guide to GCSE Music

for the **AQA** specification

by

David Bowman, Michael Burnett, Ian Burton and Bruce Cole

Rhinegold Publishing Ltd
241 Shaftesbury Avenue
London WC2H 8TF
Telephone: 01832 270333
Fax: 01832 275560
www.rhinegold.co.uk

Rhinegold Music Study Guides
(series editor: Paul Terry)

A Student's Guide to GCSE Music for the AQA Specification
A Student's Guide to GCSE Music for the Edexcel Specification
A Student's Guide to GCSE Music for the OCR Specification

A Student's Guide to AS Music for the AQA Specification
A Student's Guide to AS Music for the Edexcel Specification
A Student's Guide to AS Music for the OCR Specification

A Student's Guide to A2 Music for the AQA Specification
A Student's Guide to A2 Music for the Edexcel Specification
A Student's Guide to A2 Music for the OCR Specification

A Student's Guide to Music Technology for the Edexcel AS and A2 Specification

Rhinegold Publishing also publishes Music Teacher, Classical Music, Opera Now, Piano, Early Music Today, The Singer, British and International Music Yearbook, Music Education Yearbook, British Performing Arts Yearbook, Rhinegold Dictionary of Music in Sound.

First published 2002 in Great Britain by
Rhinegold Publishing Ltd
241 Shaftesbury Avenue
London WC2H 8TF
Telephone: 01832 270333
Fax: 01832 275560
www.rhinegold.co.uk

© Rhinegold Publishing Ltd

A Student's Guide to GCSE Music for the AQA specification
British Library Cataloguing in Publication Data.
A catalogue record for this book is available from the British Library.
ISBN 1-904226-03-5

Printed in Great Britain by Perfectaprint (UK) Ltd

Contents

The authors

David Bowman was for 20 years director of music at Ampleforth College where he still teaches. He was a chief examiner for the University of London Schools Examination Board (now Edexcel) from 1982 to 1998. David's publications include the *London Anthology of Music* (ULSEB, 1986), *Sound Matters*, (co-authored with Bruce Cole, Schott, 1989), *Aural Matters* (co-authored with Paul Terry, Schott, 1993), *Aural Matters in Practice* (co-authored with Paul Terry, Schott, 1994), *Analysis Matters* (Rhinegold, Volume 1 1997, Volume 2 1998) and numerous analytical articles for *Music Teacher*. He is a contributor to the *Collins Classical Music Encyclopedia* (2000) edited by Stanley Sadie and author of the *Rhinegold Dictionary of Music in Sound* (2002).

Michael Burnett lectures in music at the University of Surrey Roehampton where he has been involved in teacher training for almost 20 years. During that time Michael wrote and presented the BBC Schools radio programme *Music Box* for a period of ten years. He was also seconded to the Jamaica School of Music for three years. Michael's compositions and arrangements have been widely published. He is the author of three books in the Oxford Topics in Music series for 11- to 14-year-olds, and arranger of several song and instrumental collections for IMP. He was series editor of the secondary-level teaching resource *Music File*, published by Stanley Thornes (1991–1998), and regularly writes on music for the *Times Educational Supplement*.

Ian Burton is senior lecturer in music education at Huddersfield University. He previously ran the PGCE secondary music course at Bath Spa University College, and was director of music for many years in comprehensive schools and colleges. He has been principal examiner in composing for OCR A-level music and is a subject adviser for AQA GCSE music. He was involved with the development of the current A-level and GCSE music specifications, and is a regular contributor to *Music Teacher*. He is active as a composer/arranger with particular interests in creating material for use in schools.

Bruce Cole is fellow in community music at the University of York, principal examiner in composition for Edexcel and has been a scrutineer for the Qualifications and Curriculum Authority. He has taught at most levels from pre-school to postgraduate, and his work as a composer includes rock musicals, orchestral commissions and scores for film, television, theatre and dance. He is the author of *The Composer's Handbook*, the co-author (with David Bowman) of *Sound Matters* and a member of the *Music Education Research* editorial board.

Acknowledgements

The authors would like to thank Peter Owens and Julia Winterson of Peters Edition, Hallam Bannister, Daniel Burnett, Lucien Jenkins, Elizabeth Ling, Robert Mason, David McCord, Paul Terry, Abigail Walmsley, Alison Welch and Adrian York for their advice and support during the preparation of this guide. Nevertheless if any errors have been made it is only right to state that these are the responsibilities of the authors.

Introduction

This is a guide specially written for pupils studying for the AQA GCSE in music. You're still going to need to go to your lessons: we are offering you some extra help, not a substitute for what your teachers have to offer. There are four parts to GCSE music, each of which accounts for 25% of the total mark for the subject. Your teacher will assess your work for the first two parts and the marks will be checked by AQA. Your work for the third and fourth parts will be marked directly by AQA examiners.

1. Coursework Composing

You will have to compose two pieces, at least one of which should be based on Area of Study 3, *Music for Special Events*. Your compositions should be submitted as scores, with recordings wherever possible, or else recordings with detailed notes.

2. Coursework Performing

You will have to perform one solo piece and one ensemble piece, both of which must be recorded. The performances can take place at any time during the course.

3. Integrated Assignment

You will have to compose a third piece, based on one of the **other** Areas of Study (1, 2, 4 or 5) listed in the margin. This has to be written to a brief (ie detailed instructions) set by AQA in the spring term of your exam year. You submit this piece as a score with/ without annotation together with a recorded realisation and an evaluation. You will have to answer questions about this composition in a ½ hour exam in the final summer term.

Areas of Study
1. Music for Film
2. Music for Dance
3. Music for Special Events
4. Orchestral Landmarks
5. The Popular Song since 1960

4. Listening Test

This is a 1¼-hour exam at the end of the course, in which you will have to answer questions about recorded examples of music that come from all five Areas of Study. **The examples are most unlikely to come from specific pieces that you have studied in here or in *AQAA* although they will be similar.**

The questions might require you to:

✦ identify instruments

✦ recognise types and dates of music

✦ spot technical features in the work

✦ make comparisons between pieces.

You may also be asked to notate rhythms and/or pitches, and to identify chord changes and/or cadences.

AQAA stands for *AQA Anthology of Music*, published by Peters Edition. We have used that anthology as the basis of many of the Listening questions at the end of each Area of Study chapter.

Later in this guide we will look in more detail at the requirements for all four of these parts and explore ways to help you get the best possible marks.

Understanding music

This chapter covers some important terms and concepts that you will encounter during your course. Some of the points, particularly on keys and chords, may seem very difficult at first so don't try to work through the entire chapter in one go – use it as a reference source whenever you need to. Don't forget that the purpose of music theory is not to give you things to learn for homework but to help you become a better listener, performer and composer.

You will undoubtedly encounter many musical terms that are new to you. These will make much more sense if you understand the *sounds* to which they refer. Don't just rely on learning definitions, but play or sing the examples and use them in your own composing. Understanding musical terminology will help you convey to fellow musicians (even examiners!) complex ideas in just a word or two, rather than having to use long descriptions. But remember that musical terminology must be understood thoroughly and used correctly if it is to make sense.

Clefs

You will probably be familiar with the **treble clef**. Its symbol ($\oint$) developed from an elaborate letter G which wraps around the line of the stave that represents the pitch G above middle C.

You will also encounter the **bass clef**. Its symbol ($\mathcal{9}$) developed from a letter F which wraps around the line of the stave that represents the pitch F below middle C.

The treble clef is used for melody instruments such as the flute, oboe, clarinet, saxophone, trumpet, horn, violin and recorder, as well as for treble and alto voices. The bass clef is used for bass voices and bass instruments such as the bassoon, trombone, tuba, cello and double bass. Keyboard instruments and the harp use both clefs.

The **vocal tenor clef** is easy to understand. It looks the same as a treble clef but with a small figure *8* at the bottom. This indicates that the music sounds an octave lower than the equivalent treble clef notes. It is used for tenor voices (hence its name) and for lead-guitar parts. Sometimes these parts are written in the normal treble clef, it being taken for granted that tenor singers and guitarists know that their part sounds an octave lower than written.

The symbol for the C clef ($\mathbb{B}$) developed from a letter C which wraps around the line of the stave that represents middle C. It can appear on the middle line of the stave, in which case it is known as the alto clef. Viola parts use this version of the C clef. It can also appear on the fourth line up of the stave, in which case it is known as the tenor clef. The tenor clef is used for the higher notes of the cello, double bass, bassoon and trombone. You will not need to become expert in reading the C clef unless you choose to use it in your compositions.

The examples *above left* show the first three notes of *Three Blind Mice* in all five of these clefs. Notice that all five end on middle C and they all sound exactly the same. The last stave in the example uses a percussion clef. It doesn't indicate pitches at all, but it allows a stave to be used for a variety of drum-kit sounds of indefinite pitch.

To understand this chapter you will need to be able to read simple music notation. If you find this difficult try to spend some time early in the course getting yourself up to speed. There are many books on music notation and theory – your teacher will be able to suggest one that is appropriate. There are also websites and CD-Roms on the subject and these often allow you to test yourself as you go. The best way of all though, is to identify gaps in your knowledge and then ask your teacher for help. They won't mind – in fact they will be delighted if you are interested in improving your skills. And your teacher can explain things in the way you are most likely to understand if you find a concept hard to grasp. Remember that the best way to practise music-reading skills, and to explore new music, is to do as much sight-reading as you can manage.

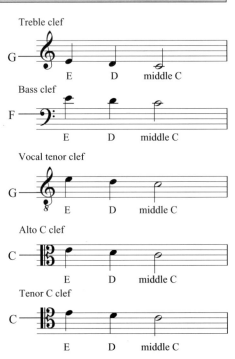

Major scales and major keys

Scales are one of the main building-blocks in many types of music. We may not enjoy playing them, but they are essential in building up an understanding of how music works.

An interval is the distance between two pitches. The smallest interval normally used in western music is a semitone. On the keyboard diagram *below* there is a semitone between notes 1 and 2, and another semitone between notes 2 and 3. The interval between notes 1 and 3 is therefore two semitones, or a tone.

'Semi' means 'half', so a semitone is half a tone.

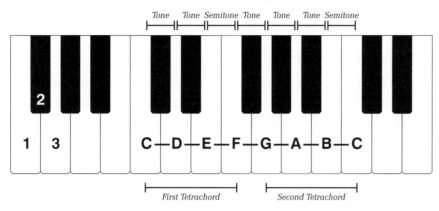

Now look at the scale of C major shown on this diagram. There is no black note between E and F, or between B and C. This is because these notes are already only a semitone apart.

Can you see the pattern of intervals in this scale? It starts with a group of four notes (known as a tetrachord) that are separated by the intervals tone–tone–semitone, and it ends with another group of four notes in exactly the same pattern. The last note of the first tetrachord and the first note of the second are a tone apart. So the entire eight-note scale makes the pattern:

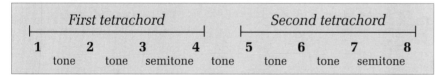

It may seem complicated but once you understand the pattern you can construct every major scale there is!

Let's put theory into practice and use the formula to construct a major scale starting on G. The first tetrachord will be G–A–B–C, which happens to be the same as the second tetrachord of C major (see *right*). We know that the other tetrachord must start a tone above the last note of the first tetrachord. To keep to the invariable tone–tone–semitone pattern it will have to consist of the notes D–E–F♯–G.

The important difference between the notes of C major and G major is that the former contains F♮ while the latter contains F♯. Keys which have most of their notes in common like this are described as being closely related.

Now try constructing a scale of D major. It begins with the second tetrachord of G major, shown *right* (D–E–F♯–G) and it ends with the tetrachord A–B–C♯–D. This scale is closely related to G major (only one pitch, C♯, is different) but less closely related to C major (where two pitches, F♯ and C♯, are different).

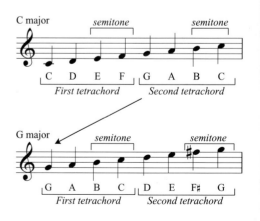

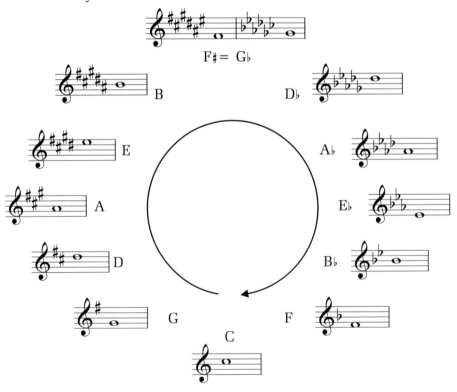

F major

First tetrachord Second tetrachord

semitone   semitone

F G A B♭ C D E F

Follow the pattern one more time and write out a major scale starting on A. You should find that this time you need three sharps. Do you notice that every time you start a new scale on the fifth note of the previous scale, it needs one more sharp?

Now try writing out the major scale that starts on the fourth note of C major (F). In order to maintain our usual pattern you should end up with the scale of F major shown *left*. We can see that it is closely related to C major because both keys have all notes except one (B♭) in common. Repeat the process by starting a scale on the fourth note of F major (B♭), and you should find that the new scale needs two flats (B♭ and E♭). You have probably guessed by now … every time you start a new scale on the fourth note of the previous scale, it needs one more flat.

Rather than writing a sharp or flat before each note that needs one it is more convenient to use a key signature at the start of each stave to indicate the sharps or flats required.

There are 12 possible major keys in all, and you can see their relationships in the following diagram. Keys next to each other in the circle are closely related. Notice that, at the top of the circle, the notes in the key of F♯ major (six sharps) sound the same as the notes in the key of G♭ major (six flats). They are said to be enharmonic equivalents, which means that they sound the same but are written differently.

Notice that if you go round the circle clockwise from C major you add a sharp for each new key until you get to six sharps. It is then more sensible to use flats – and you must deduct a flat for each new key until you get back to C major.

When you write out a key signature the sharps or flats are always used in the fixed order shown above. If you need to use the bass clef, follow the order given in the example shown *left*.

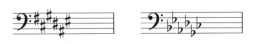

Scale degrees

It is often more convenient to refer, not to individual note names, but to the function of each note in a scale. For example the first note of a major (or minor) scale is always the key note, or tonic, whatever key the music is in. Here are the technical names for each degree of the scale – Roman numerals are often used instead of the technical names:

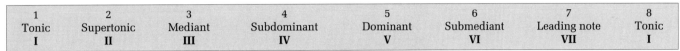

1	2	3	4	5	6	7	8
Tonic	Supertonic	Mediant	Subdominant	Dominant	Submediant	Leading note	Tonic
I	II	III	IV	V	VI	VII	I

Earlier we saw how one of the most closely related keys to the tonic is the one a 5th higher than the tonic – so you won't be surprised to see that V is called the dominant. In the example below we can see that the dominant note of G is D. Similarly, the dominant key of G major is D major.

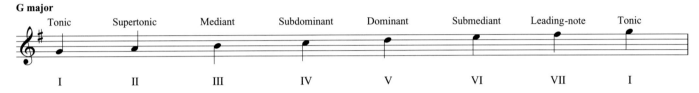

G major

Tonic	Supertonic	Mediant	Subdominant	Dominant	Submediant	Leading-note	Tonic
I	II	III	IV	V	VI	VII	I

Test yourself on major scales and keys

1. Write out the scale of E♭ major in the treble clef. Which note is the dominant of E♭ major?

2. Write out the scale of A major in the bass clef. Which note is the subdominant of A major?

Minor scales and minor keys

Paired with every major key is a minor key with the same key signature. This **relative minor** is another key that is closely associated with the original tonic. It always starts on the submediant (sixth note) of its related major key. So the relative minor of C major starts on A and is called A minor. Instead of counting up six steps to the submediant to find the starting note, you may prefer to think of it as two scale steps below the tonic:

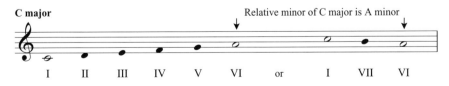

C major   Relative minor of C major is A minor

| I | II | III | IV | V | VI | or | I | VII | VI |

We can say that A minor is the relative minor of C major, or we can say that C major is the relative major of A minor. The starting note (or tonic) of all other minor keys is worked out in exactly the same way. So, what is the relative minor of each of the following keys: G major, D major, F major, B♭ major, A major, E♭ major?

Minor keys are sometimes misleadingly described as sad and major keys as happy. Fast music in a minor key can sound brilliant, stormy or angry, just as slow music in a major key can sound tragic or nostalgic. If asked to identify a key as being major or minor in a listening test you will need to listen very carefully to the relationship between notes and not rely on simplistic descriptions of this kind.

Minor scales come in several different versions. The easiest one to start with is what is known as the natural minor. It uses exactly the same notes as its relative major, but because it starts on a different tonic, the intervals between the notes in the scale are different:

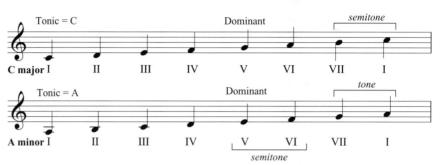

These differences are most obvious at the top end of the scale. Play or sing several scales of C major, each time stopping on note VII. You will undoubtedly feel that the scale sounds incomplete unless the last note rises a semitone to finish on C, the tonic. This tendency is so strong that it gives note VII its technical name of leading-note – the note that needs to lead to the tonic.

The natural minor scale ends with an interval of a tone, and so doesn't display this tendency to the same extent. Repeat the experiment with the second example above, stopping on VII, and you will find that the need for it to rise to the tonic is less strongly felt.

The natural minor does not convey a strong sense of tonality (by which is meant a sense of key in which the tonic is the most important note). In order to establish a strong sense of key, the minor scale needs to end with the same rising semitone between VII and I that is found in major keys. The easy way to achieve this is to raise note VII by a semitone, but this then creates a rather odd-sounding interval between notes VI and VII:

If you have had to prepare scales for exams you may recognise that this example is the **harmonic minor scale** – it is better suited for harmonising music than for use in melodies because of the awkward melodic interval between notes VI and VII.

To avoid this awkward interval, note VI is also often raised by a semitone, giving the following version of a minor scale:

You may recognise that this example comes from the **melodic minor** scale, which is better suited for melody writing. It has the pattern shown here when ascending, but it uses the natural-minor scale pattern when descending.

In a minor-key piece you may thus find notes VI and VII in both normal and raised versions:

Vivaldi, Op.3 No.8

However the raised version of the leading note followed by the tonic (shown bracketed above) is needed to convey a firm sense of minor tonality, and the presence of this pattern is a clear indicator that the key is minor.

Notice that raising the pitch of notes VI and VII does not always mean using a sharp. If either of these notes is normally flat, then you will need a natural, not a sharp, to raise its pitch by a semitone:

C minor: I   II   III   IV   V   VI   VII   I

Try to build-up speed and accuracy in recognising keys, scales and the degrees of the scale – it will help you understand later topics, particularly chords, very much more easily.

Test yourself on minor scales and keys

1. Name the relative minor of F major and state the pitch of its raised leading note. ....

2. Write out an ascending scale of B minor in the treble clef, using the raised form of the sixth and seventh degrees of this scale.

3. Name the key of the following passage of music: ....

Vivaldi, Op.3 No.2

4. Name the relative major of F♯ minor: ....

Other scales and modes

The **pentatonic scale** is a five-note scale found in folk music in many different parts of the world. The major pentaonic scale uses notes 1–2–3–5–6 of the major scale (see *right*). If you play a scale on just the black notes of a keyboard, starting on F♯, you will hear the major pentatonic scale in F♯. The minor pentatonic scale uses notes 1, 3, 4, 5 and 7 of the natural minor scale (see *right*).

The pentatonic scale is very useful when you first start composing because, since the scale doesn't include any semitones, it is possible to combine melodic lines and use simple drone accompaniments without creating harsh dissonances.

Major pentatonic scale starting on C

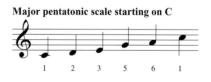

1   2   3   5   6   1

Minor pentatonic scale starting on C

1   3   4   5   7   1

Unlike the pentatonic scale, the **chromatic scale** consists entirely of semitones, 12 of them to the octave:

Chromatic scale

The **whole-tone scale** proceeds entirely in steps of a tone:

Whole-tone scale

A **mode** is simply a set of notes. The major scale is one kind of mode and the natural minor scale that we saw on page 10 is another – indeed, it is the same as the aeolian mode printed *left*. This example shows three of the most common modes. At first sight they may look like major scales, but the significant difference is the relationship of the notes within the mode. Notice that none of those printed here ends with a semitone between its last two notes – one of the characteristic features of a major scale. For GCSE you will not be required to distinguish between the different types of mode, but you might be expected to recognise that a passage is modal.

Aeolian mode

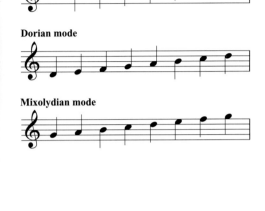

Dorian mode

Mixolydian mode

Intervals

Remember that an interval is the distance between two notes. If the two notes occur simultaneously they form a harmonic interval. If they occur in succession they form a melodic interval, either ascending or descending. All are described in the same way, by counting the letter names from the lower note to the higher note. Always count the lower note as 1. The intervals shown *left* are all 5ths.

However describing intervals by number alone is insufficient. For instance, the interval from D to F is a 3rd – but so is the interval from D to F♯ and they are clearly not the same. We need to add a description of the 'quality' of the interval in order to be more precise.

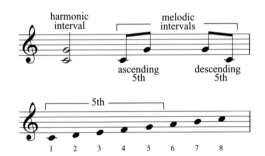

harmonic interval   melodic intervals   ascending 5th   descending 5th

5th   1 2 3 4 5 6 7 8

To do this, imagine that the lower note of the interval is the key note (or tonic) of a major scale. If the upper note belongs to that scale the interval will be named as follows:

| (perfect) unison | major 2nd | major 3rd | perfect 4th | perfect 5th | major 6th | major 7th | (perfect) octave | major 9th |

In every major and minor scale, you'll find that the intervals between the tonic and fourth, fifth and octave degrees above are called 'perfect'.

If the interval is one semitone smaller than a major interval, it is a minor interval. That gives us the following possibilities:

| minor 2nd | minor 3rd | | minor 6th | minor 7th | | minor 9th |

The minor 2nd sounds the same as a semitone and the major 2nd sounds the same as a tone. Notice how you have to stagger the note heads when writing these small intervals on a single stave.

If an interval is one semitone smaller than a minor or perfect interval, it is diminished. And if an interval is one semitone larger than a major or perfect interval, it is augmented:

| major 7th | minor 7th | diminished 7th | perfect 5th | diminished 5th | perfect 4th | augmented 4th | major 2nd | augmented 2nd |

The diminished 5th and the augmented 4th sound the same when heard in isolation. Both consist of an interval of three tones, and each is therefore often called a **tritone**.

Notice that you can alter the quality of an interval by changing either of its notes. The diminished 7th in the previous example is a semitone smaller than the minor 7th because its lower note has been raised by a semitone.

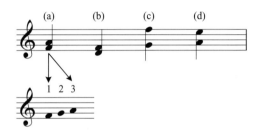

> ### Naming intervals: a summary
> First work out the number of the interval. Next decide if the upper note is in the major scale of which the lower note is the tonic. If it is, the interval will be major or perfect. If not, the following rules usually help:
> If the interval is a semitone smaller than a major interval, it is minor.
> If the interval is a semitone larger than a major or perfect interval, it is augmented.
> If the interval is a semitone smaller than a minor or perfect interval, it is diminished.

One of the most confusing things about naming intervals is the fact that minor intervals occur in major keys, and major intervals occur in minor keys.

Let's see how this works in practice with the examples shown *right*. First work out the number of the interval, remembering to count the lower note as 1. Interval (a) is a 3rd (F=1, G=2, A=3). Next imagine the lower note (F) to be the tonic. Does the upper note (A) occur in the key of F major? Yes! So this is a major 3rd.

Example (b) is also a 3rd. Imagine the lower note (D) to be the tonic. Does the upper note (F) occur in the key of D major? No! The third note in D major is F♯, but here we have an F♮ – so interval (b) is a semitone less than a major 3rd. It is a minor 3rd.

Now work out interval (c). The lower note is G. Does the upper note (F) occur in G major? If it doesn't, this cannot be a major interval. What interval is it? Work out interval (d) for yourself.

Test yourself on intervals

Write the named harmonic interval by writing a note *above* each of the following notes.

(a)	(b)	(c)	(d)	(e)	(f)	(g)
Minor 3rd	Perfect 4th	Minor 7th	Perfect 5th	Octave	Minor 2nd	Minor 3rd

Triads

The simplest type of chord is the **triad**. It consists of three pitches: the note on which the chord is based (the **root**), along with a 3rd and 5th above it. Here are the triads on each note of a C major scale:

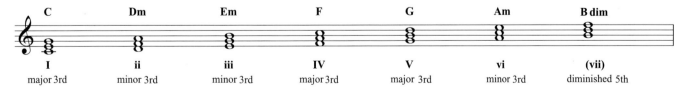

C	Dm	Em	F	G	Am	B dim
I	ii	iii	IV	V	vi	(vii)
major 3rd	minor 3rd	minor 3rd	major 3rd	major 3rd	minor 3rd	diminished 5th

Triads can be described by using the technical names or the Roman numerals that are used for naming the degrees of the scale. For instance, in the key of C major the dominant chord (chord V) is simply the triad on the dominant note (G).

Upper-case Roman numerals (ie I, II, etc) are often used to indicate major triads while lower-case Roman numerals (ie i, ii, etc) can be used to indicate minor triads.

Look carefully at the interval between the root and third of each chord. In chords I, IV and V the middle note is a major 3rd above the root. These are therefore major chords, and are known as the three primary triads. In chords ii, iii and vi the middle note is a minor 3rd above the root. These are known as minor chords.

The interval between the root and top note is a perfect 5th in every triad except vii. Here the outer interval is a diminished 5th and this triad is therefore known as a diminished triad.

In pop and jazz it is more usual to notate chords by writing the letter name of the root above the stave. A single capital letter indicates a major chord. A lower case 'm' after a capital letter indicates a minor chord, while 'dim' indicates a diminished triad.

The notes of a chord can be positioned in any octave, with any spacing and with notes duplicated. All of the chords shown *left* are G major – even the last one can be assumed to be G major, despite the fact that one of the notes (the 5th, D) is omitted.

Notice that the root of the triad (G) is the lowest note of all five chords in this example. When, as here, the root is also the bass note the chord is said to be in **root position**.

Inversions

If a chord is arranged so that the root is *not* the lowest note it is said to be inverted. If the 3rd is in the bass the triad is said to be in **first inversion**. This is indicated by adding the letter 'b' to the appropriate Roman numeral (see *left*: a root-position triad should have the letter 'a' after the Roman numeral, but it is usually omitted). You may also see a first inversion expressed as $\frac{6}{3}$, indicating that the upper two notes are a 6th and a 3rd above the bass.

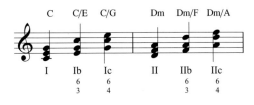

If the 5th is in the bass the triad is said to be in **second inversion** and this is indicated by adding the letter 'c' to the appropriate Roman numeral. You may see a second inversion expressed as $\frac{6}{4}$, indicating that the upper notes are a 6th and a 4th above the bass.

It should now be clear that however the upper notes of a chord are arranged, the bass note is especially important. This is also true if you use chord symbols other than Roman numerals. If the bass note is not the root, write an oblique stroke after the chord symbol and then name the bass note required: eg C/E indicates a chord of C major with E in the bass (in other words, a first inversion).

More elaborate chords can be formed by adding a 7th above the root – you will often see chords V and II embellished in this way, as shown *left*. If you add a diminished 7th to chord VII you will form a dramatic chord known as a diminished seventh.

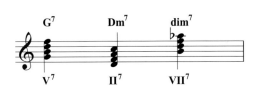

It is also possible to add other notes to triads (such as 2nds or 9ths) and to make chromatic alterations to one or more of the notes of the triad. However while such techniques are well worth exploring when composing, they are beyond the requirements of GCSE.

Melodic decoration

If melodies only used notes from the accompanying chords they would sound very dull, so basic harmony notes are frequently enlivened with various types of melodic decoration. These often create a momentary dissonance (ie a clash) with the underlying harmony.

These decorative (or 'unessential') notes may be **diatonic**, which means they use notes from the prevailing key, or they may be **chromatic**, meaning that they use notes from outside the prevailing key. And, although we have called this section melodic decoration, these embellishments may occur in the melody, bass or an inner part.

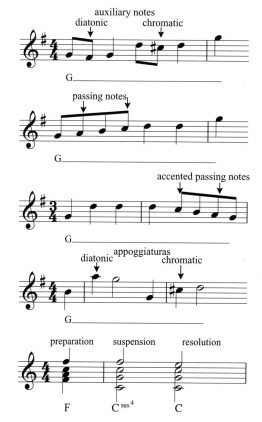

An **auxiliary note** lies a tone or a semitone above or below a harmony note and returns to it. A **passing note** moves by step between two harmony notes that are a third apart. Passing notes normally occur on weak beats. If they occur on strong beats they will be much more obviously dissonant and are then known as accented passing notes.

An **appoggiatura** is a dissonance that is approached by a leap. The tension created is released when the appoggiatura 'resolves' by moving to a harmony note.

A **suspension** starts with a consonant note which is then sustained or repeated (ie suspended) over a change of harmony, causing a discord. The discord then resolves to a harmony note, usually by moving downwards by step. In most cases the suspension actually replaces one of the harmony notes. For instance in the example *right*, the normal 3rd of a C-major chord (E) has been temporarily replaced by F, a 4th above C. In pop and jazz, suspensions are often treated as chords in their own right and are notated with a separate chord symbol ($C^{sus\,4}$ in this case).

Figuration

If chords were always used as plain blocks of notes music would sound very boring. Even in a simple accompanied melody composers usually make the accompaniment more interesting by devising patterns from the chord notes. These patterns are known as figures, and can be adapted to fit changes in the chords. The example *right* shows just five ways of devising a figure from a C-major chord. Pattern (a) is a simple arpeggio figure, while (b) is a broken-chord figure known as an Alberti bass (named after a composer who over-used this type of figuration). The syncopation in pattern (c) gives this figure a more urgent feel. Patterns (d) and (e) both include unessential notes.

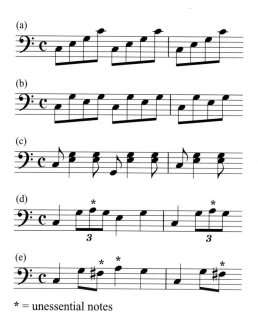

* = unessential notes

Motifs, phrases and cadences

A **motif** is a short melodic or rhythmic idea that is distinctive enough to maintain its identity despite being changed in various ways. It is often the basic cell from which much longer musical ideas are constructed, as in this example by Mozart:

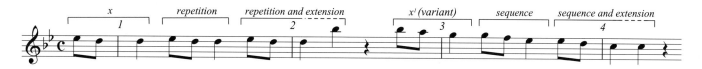

The opening motif (x) features a rhythm (♪♪ | ♩) and a falling semitone. First it is repeated exactly, then it is repeated and extended by an upward leap and a rest. Next it is adapted so that there is a fall to the third note (x^1). This variant is then treated in

sequence (which means the immediate repetition of an idea at a different pitch). The last appearance is again extended to match the rhythm (but not the rising leap) of the first extension. In Mozart's Symphony No 41 the entire **phrase** quoted above is then repeated in sequence a step lower, creating a perfectly balanced pair of phrases.

The phrase begins on the last beat of a bar. An opening on a weak beat like this is known as an anacrusis. It means that the music starts with an incomplete bar and the final bar of the example is shortened to balance. The example thus contains 16 beats in all and we can still refer to it as being a four-bar phrase, even though it doesn't fit into four complete bars. Notice how bars are numbered when there is an anacrusic start – bar 1 is the first *complete* bar.

Phrases often end with a **cadence** – a point of repose, rather like punctuation in a sentence. The perfect cadence (chords V–I) gives a sense of completion, rather like a full stop at the end of a sentence. The imperfect cadence (an ending on chord V) sounds open and incomplete – more like a comma after a phrase in a sentence:

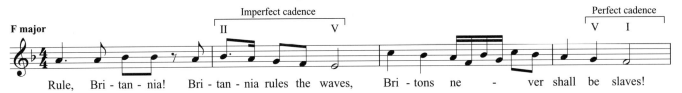

Rule, Bri - tan - nia! Bri - tan - nia rules the waves, Bri - tons ne - ver shall be slaves!

Note that chord V in an imperfect cadence can be preceded by any suitable chord (I, II or IV are the most usual).

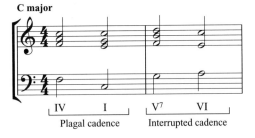

IV   I   V⁷   VI

Plagal cadence   Interrupted cadence

Two other cadences you may encounter are illustrated *left*. The plagal cadence consists of chords IV–I and is often associated with a sung 'Amen' in church music. The interrupted cadence begins with chord V (or V⁷) like a perfect cadence, but it ends with almost any chord other than I – in other words, the expected perfect cadence is interrupted by an unexpected chord.

Modulation

The perfect cadence, particularly in the form V⁷–I, has an important role in defining the key. Chord V⁷ includes the leading note, which tends to want to rise to the tonic in chord I, while the seventh of chord V⁷ tends to want to fall to the third in chord I. These chords totally define a key. Look at the melody shown *left*, which clearly outlines a perfect cadence. The chord of C⁷ includes B♭, so the key must be a flat key, but it also includes E♮. There are only two keys with this combination, F major and F minor. And when the 7th (B♭) drops to A♮ in the tonic chord we know that the key cannot be F minor – it can only be F major.

V⁷   I

When you see accidentals in a passage of music, they can have any of the following functions:

◆ they may be the sixth and/or seventh degrees of a minor scale
◆ they may indicate that the music has modulated (changed key)
◆ they may be chromatic notes which have no effect on the key.

The role of the perfect cadence in defining key will enable us to differentiate between these different functions of accidentals. Look at the following melody by Sousa:

When you see an accidental, ask yourself if it might be a leading note – if it is, the tonic will be a semitone higher and you would expect to see a perfect cadence in this key. So, the presence of G♯ might suggest the key of A minor, and F♯ might suggest G minor. But there are no perfect cadences in either of these keys.

There are only two different chords, C⁷ and F, and these make a clear perfect cadence in F major in bars 5–8. The music is therefore in the key of F major, and G♯ and F♯ are both chromatic notes.

Next look at this simplified version of a minuet by Mozart. It also starts in F major, as confirmed by the perfect cadence (C⁷–F) in bars 3–4. The first accidental is B♮ in bar 5. Is this merely chromatic or does it signify a modulation? As always, test to see if it is a leading note (eg of C major) by looking for a perfect cadence in this new key. This time there are perfect cadences in the new key, in bars 5–6 (G⁷–C) and again in bars 7–8 (G–C). So B♮ is not a chromatic note – the music does indeed modulate to the key of C major.

Remember, for a modulation to take place you should expect to see not only accidentals that reflect the new key, but also a perfect cadence in the new key.

Time names

You will probably already know the names given to lengths and rests, but you should be aware that AQA require you to know both the British terms (such as crotchet) and the American terms (such as quarter note). Here are the two systems compared:

Notes					
Lengths in crotchets	4	2	1	½	¼
Rests					
British names	Semibreve	Minim	Crotchet	Quaver	Semiquaver
American names	Whole note	Half note	Quarter note	8th note	16th note

Performing

Coursework Performing accounts for 25% of the total marks for AQA's GCSE music. You will need to perform two different pieces, one a solo and the other an ensemble item. You are only allowed to offer one solo and one ensemble item, but they can be on different instruments if you wish. These performances count as coursework. This means you can do them at any time during the course, although your teacher will need to be present when the performances take place. You have the right to do your performances as many times as you like and to pick your best work to count for the exam. Get used to recording all the performances that you do. This will mean that:

In this section, the word 'instrument' includes singing.

◆ you can listen to and think about your playing/singing

◆ you will have captured any really special performances and can use them for your GCSE.

Some students enjoy performing very much but others get extremely nervous. If you are somebody who does get nervous then take every opportunity to perform as much as you can, as this will help you to cope with your nerves. Your GCSE performances could be in front of an audience, or could be in a recording studio session: choose the location that suits you best.

Performing opportunities

You may have tuition on your instrument outside of school lessons, or it may be that all of your performing takes place in school. In either case your GCSE course should provide you with plenty of opportunities to make music, both on your own and with other people. You can practise your performing skills by:

There are also opportunities to perform as part of the Integrated Assignment. See the chapter on pages 34–41.

◆ trying out your solo and ensemble pieces and receiving feedback from your teacher and other students

◆ performing music from the Areas of Study

◆ composing music for yourself and other members of your GCSE group to perform

◆ performing or recording 'Music for Special Events' compositions by other GCSE students

◆ improvising, on your own or with others.

If you have used printed music for your performance, your teacher will need a photocopy of this music to send to the exam board.

It is important to think carefully about what music to perform for GCSE. Your teacher will be able to give you help and advice, but you should take the initiative in finding pieces for yourself. Try to choose music that includes enough variety (of mood, speed, texture, dynamics and so on) for you to demonstrate your musical ability. The pieces that you choose should allow you to show technical and expressive control as a performer as well as an understanding of the music you present. Remember that some types of music, such as technical studies and easy arrangements, may focus on only a limited range of techniques and may not give you much of a chance to show your all-round skills as a performer.

The technical difficulty of the music you choose needs careful thought. Easy pieces played musically are much more likely to be successful than difficult pieces marred by hesitations and breakdowns. Whatever your technical standard it is better to choose music that you can perform with confidence than to attempt a difficult work which stretches your technique to its limit.

Your teacher will assess the performances that you do for your GCSE coursework. A selection of recordings from your GCSE group will then be sent to AQA to make sure that all teachers are marking to the same standard.

Assessment

Solo Performing

You will need to perform one solo piece. Your solo performing is marked in four categories:

Accuracy of pitch and rhythm	8 marks
Demand	6 marks
Interpretative qualities	8 marks
Expressive qualities	8 marks
Total	30 marks

If the performance is out of tune, the rhythm is hesitant or the presentation totally breaks down, it will be very difficult to gain many marks for accuracy of pitch and rhythm.

Accuracy of pitch and rhythm

Marks awarded for demand depend on the difficulty of the music that you perform. If you choose a piece that is hard you get more credit for it. Does this mean that you should always play the hardest piece that you possibly can? No! Every year some GCSE students make this mistake, and perform a piece that they can only just get through. The danger is that you will be so concerned with getting the notes right that you have no time to think about making the performance musical. Try to perform music that gives you technical challenges but that also allows you to show your musicality. Remember that music which is too difficult will make you very nervous – and if you are worried it will be even harder to perform well.

Demand

It is worth thinking about the fact that over half of the marks for solo performing are for interpretation and expression. This makes it even more important that you are in control of the notes and rhythms of your piece so that you can concentrate on showing your musicianship. It also means that you should choose pieces to perform that allow you to demonstrate these qualities.

Interpretative and expressive qualities

Try out your performances in front of friends and ask them if the performance came over musically.

What are expressive qualities? It is probably easier to recognise these in a good performance than to describe them in words. Most good performers give the impression that they are communicating what the music is all about. They give the sense that they have something to say about the music, that they really believe in it and that they want to persuade the audience to feel the same way.

Different pieces require different approaches and this leads on to interpretative qualities. The sort of expression that might be appropriate for a performance of a keyboard piece by Mozart would

Warning. Photocopying any part of this book without permission is illegal.

Performing 19

not be appropriate for a performance of 'My Heart Will Go On' from *Titanic*, and vice-versa.

Focus on the detail throughout the music. Rather than thinking of a passage as merely 'sad' decide if you want to make it tragic, solemn, angry or doom-laden. If it is a dance, how do you make it dance? If it is a waltz, how do you create the feel of a glittering ballroom? Try to convey the moods you intend in your interpretation of the piece – whether it be the moonlit night of a nocturne or the smoky surroundings of a blues club. Never be content with merely 'getting the notes right'.

It is important to reach a view on what the music is all about and to try to communicate this to your audience. Your teacher will be able to give you help and advice on interpretation, but at GCSE level you shouldn't always rely on being told how to perform music. Start making decisions for yourself, and discuss these with your teacher. If your teacher makes particular suggestions to you about the way you should perform something ask them to explain why.

To understand the context of a piece, listen to other performers playing the music and see if you can discover whether it was written for a particular occasion and purpose, what the music communicates, what was the common musical style at the time the piece was written and so on. This will help you to develop an understanding of the music you are going to perform.

The more you know about the music, the more likely you are to be able to perform it expressively and with a real sense of style. Ask your teacher to help you find out about any performing conventions for the type of music you are going to play or sing.

Performing exercise

1. Play through all or part of *The Last Post* on any instrument.

2. *The Last Post* is a military bugle call played at the end of the day. It signals that the night sentries are at their posts and other soldiers must retire for the evening. It is also used in funeral and memorial services as a final farewell to the dead, symbolising that their duty is over. With this latter context in mind, think about how to interpret this piece expressively.

3. You should make decisions about:

   ◆ how fast to play this piece

   ◆ if and when to speed up and slow down

   ◆ whether to pause on certain notes or rests

   ◆ whether to follow the printed phrase marks

   ◆ how loud or soft to play each section – does it seem to build up or fade away at any point?

   ◆ where to breathe (if you are a wind or brass player).

4. Now perform *The Last Post* in a manner suitable for a Remembrance Day ceremony.

5. Think about pieces that you might perform for GCSE. How will you interpret the music? How can you make your performance expressive in an appropriate way for the style of the piece?

Listening

Some musicians learn by ear and others use printed music. Whichever way you work you can benefit from listening to a range of different performances of music that you intend to present. Try to get hold of two or more recordings of the same piece of music, and compare how different musicians have interpreted it. If you can't actually find a recording of the piece you are going to perform then try to find recordings of similar pieces of music. You will often find that musicians interpret the same music in very different ways.

Accompaniment

At GCSE level your solo performance can be you entirely on your own or you can be supported by an accompanying instrument. You will probably want to perform on your own if:

◆ you are a keyboard player

◆ you are playing or singing a piece designed to be performed without accompaniment (eg a folksong)

◆ you are singing and accompanying yourself on guitar or keyboard.

Many pieces do have accompaniments, and you should always perform with these otherwise a large part of the piece will be missing. It is worth giving some thought about how to provide the best backing for your solo. There are several options. You could perform with:

◆ your teacher or another pupil on piano, keyboard, guitar etc

◆ a sequenced or multi-tracked backing

◆ an ensemble or band, as long as you are able to show genuine solo performing skills which are clearly audible on the recording made for the exam.

Whatever you do, make sure that you rehearse with the accompaniment. Many GCSE students leave this until too late, and

For an example of different interpretations look at the song 'Colours of the Wind' from *Pocahontas*. This is one of the scores suggested in the Music for Film Area of Study and, like many of the Disney films, the CD contains a dramatic and a chart version of the main song. There are two very different interpretations of the same music here. Listen carefully to both versions and make a list of the ways that the song has been interpreted differently. Think about differences in tempo, instrumental backing, melody line, vocal style, phrasing, key and dynamics.

then get very confused when they try to perform against a backing that they don't know well enough. If your teacher is going to accompany you on the piano ask them to record a backing for you to rehearse to.

Ensemble Performing

In addition to the solo piece, you have to perform as a member of an ensemble. This will involve you in making music with other members of your GCSE group, or perhaps in working with a small group that rehearses outside lessons. The guidance given on how to choose pieces for your solo performance also applies to ensemble work, but there are some additional things to think about. The music you choose for ensemble performance should allow you to:

✦ perform an *individual* part in an ensemble (the part you perform should not be doubled all the way through by another performer)

✦ show genuine ensemble skills (the ability to relate to the other performers and to make appropriate adjustments to your timing, tuning and dynamics to fit in with them).

Think carefully about this. If your ensemble performance consists of you doing your own thing while the other performers just tag along, then you are unlikely to be showing the necessary skills and equally unlikely to get a good mark in this area. Choose a piece that really requires you to listen to and work with other musicians. Avoid anything that feels like another solo with accompaniment.

Ensemble performing is marked in four categories:

Accuracy of pitch and rhythm	8 marks
Demand	6 marks
Interpretative and expressive qualities	8 marks
Sense of ensemble	8 marks
Total	30 marks

Your ensemble performance is assessed in a similar way to the solo, but there is an additional category of marks given for 'sense of ensemble' (*left*). To do well in this category you will need to show a real sense of the ensemble working together as one, and an ability to accommodate the strengths and weaknesses of other performers. You need to think about balance. It's very common for some instruments to be too loud and others not to be loud enough. It is hard to get this right if you are using lots of amplification. You may need to ask a friend to tell you how the ensemble sounds to an audience. It also helps if you show that you can cope well with any difficulties that occur during the performance (for example, you might need to put in an extra bar to make up for the fact that one of the other performers comes in late).

Ensemble rehearsals

It is vitally important to rehearse your ensemble piece thoroughly with the rest of the group. This is often easier if the ensemble consists of your fellow GCSE students and you can rehearse in lesson time. If that is not the case, you will need to plan carefully. There will be times when some performers are unavoidably absent, rooms are not available, or people forget to bring their instruments or music. You should therefore plan for at least twice the number of rehearsals you think is necessary.

Ensemble rehearsals will be much more fun, and much more efficient, if all the members understand the difference between practising and rehearsing. Practising is done by each individual, before the ensemble meets for the first time while rehearsing is done by the ensemble after all of its members have learnt at least the basics of their own individual parts.

Check with your teacher that all members of the ensemble have their music well in advance so they can practise before they meet together, and that dates, times and venues of rehearsals are clearly understood – this attention to detail is all part of learning to become a good and reliable musician.

Music technology

Your solo performance can be accompanied by a backing track that you have put together using a computer or multi-track tape recorder. If you have put the backing together yourself then you can be assessed on the whole performance, both backing and solo line. You must perform one part live in front of your teacher when you are assessed.

Ensemble performing can also make use of music technology backings, but you must work as an ensemble with at least one other live performer on top of the backing. Only the live part of the performance can be assessed.

How to practise

You will do better in the performing part of your GCSE if you are able to establish effective practice routines. It is much better to organise this so that you do a little bit of practice every day rather than have a big panic a few weeks before a performance.

Plan your practice time and use it methodically. So many performances at GCSE level start off well and then break down a few bars into the piece. This is because when music students practice they nearly always start at the beginning.

Go through the piece and identify the passages that you really can't play or sing, or record yourself performing and identify places that don't sound so good. This can be painful until you get used to hearing yourself, but there is no better way of judging how your performance will come over to an audience. It is tempting to play the easy bits over and over again because they sound good, but the smart thing to do is to concentrate on the difficult bits. Learning to perform music well requires you really to think about what you are doing. Don't just go through a piece over and over again in the hope that it will get better.

It is important to practise pieces all the way through at times, as though in a performance. Students often stop when something goes wrong and then either retake that little bit or start again at the beginning in the hope that it will go better the second time. If you always practise in this way there is a real danger that when the actual performance comes and something does go wrong that the whole piece will break down. Being able to keep going while performing is a skill that you can develop. If you play a wrong note or chord, make yourself keep going and try to keep the overall rhythm of the piece flowing. At all costs, don't ruin a performance by worrying about the fact that something has gone wrong. You need all your concentration to make sure the rest goes well.

When you have made a list of sections of a piece that you can't cope with yet, try and work out what the problem is:

◆ if you are a keyboard player it may be that you need to work out the fingering for a particular passage

◆ if you are a singer it may be that you need to work out where you are going to breathe

◆ if you are a guitarist (or pianist) it may be that there is a particularly difficult chord change requiring you to practise an awkward shift of hand position

◆ if you are a brass player you may need to do lip-strengthening exercises to reach high notes.

In each of these cases if you can identify what the problem is then you can start to work out solutions.

Try to practise in the place where you will be performing. Different rooms make a big difference to the way your music sounds.

If you are a wind or string player make sure you practise tuning your instrument to your accompanist's instrument or to the instruments of other members of an ensemble. Wind/brass players need to warm up before tuning; string players should check all the strings. Spend some time getting this right – few things are more painful than musicians being out of tune.

Composing

Requirements

Aim to complete most of the work on your compositions by the start of the spring term of your examination year: you will need time to work on the integrated assignment over the final few months of the course.

See the chapter on *Music for Special Events* (page 70).

The acoustics of the space where you are to perform can have a big impact on how your music will sound and you should think about this while you are composing. In a dry acoustic (or outside) instruments/ voices may sound rather thin and you might need to double up parts or use amplification. In a resonant space (such as a sports hall or church) fast music might sound muddled due to the echo.

Special events that might involve music	
Religious and cultural events	Christmas, Diwali, Thanksgiving
Festivals	Chinese New Year (or any other New Year celebration) Bonfire Night, Saint Patrick's Day (or any other Saint), Mardi Gras (or any other carnival), harvest festival
Family	Births, christenings, Bar Mitzvah, confirmations, weddings, anniversaries, funerals
School and work	Prize giving, opening a new building, unveiling a statue, welcoming a special visitor, special assembly, school disco, sports day
Political and state occasions	A campaign song, music for a rally, an anthem for peace, an independence day march, a piece for Remembrance Sunday
Royal events	Jubilees, visits and tours, state opening of parliament, trooping the colour
Sport	A World Cup song, an Olympic hymn, music for a dressage event, music for a gymnastics display

You will probably compose a number of pieces during your GCSE course, but you are required to submit *two* pieces for assessment. One must be based on the Area of Study: Music for Special Events. The other composition can be based on another Area of Study or on some totally different idea that interests you. Your teacher will tell you when your work needs to be ready: this is likely to be no later than the start of May in your examination year.

Composition 1: Music for Special Events

One of your compositions needs to be designed for a special event. It could be an imaginary event, but you will learn much more if you compose for a real one and become involved in the performance of your music at the event. This way you will face the challenges of being a real composer by finding out about the nature of the event and negotiating with the organisers about the suitability of the music and any limitations that might be involved. Having a fixed performance date is also a real incentive to get on with your work!

The first step will be to identify a suitable special event. What sort of event is it? What views do the organisers have about the type and length of music that would be suitable? What will the audience be like? What performers will be available? What experience do they have? How much space is there to perform (and are there electrical sockets if you need them)? What are the acoustics like? When you have collected this information you can use it to write a brief for your composition (see *below*).

Think about the type of music you feel most confident composing while trying to identify a suitable special event (see *left*). If you are a brass player you might look for an event that involves a fanfare. If you enjoy song writing you might look for events where a commemorative song would be appropriate. Whatever you choose to compose, make sure you understand the nature of the event and how you can make your music relevant.

Writing the brief for composition 1

Your composition must be based on a brief, a statement of what the piece is meant to achieve. Being able to meet a brief is an essential part of the composer's job. The brief for your compositions can be written by yourself or your teacher.

If you write the brief for composition 1, it is likely to be based around the research that you have done into the demands of the relevant special event. Make it clear that you have thought carefully about how to design your piece to be appropriate for the event and performers. It is important to take care to work to a detailed, realistic brief, because:

✦ you will be assessed on the extent to which your composition meets the demands of the brief

✦ once the brief for composition 1 has been designed, you mustn't change the nature of the special event to fit your composition.

Sample brief: Music for a Special Event

◆ the brief is to compose a celebratory piece to accompany a dance display at the school's summer fair (held in a marquee on the school field)

Talk to the dancers about suitable speeds and rhythms for dance.

◆ the theme of the fair is 'Caribbean Carnival', so the piece should use some Caribbean rhythms (perhaps calypso or reggae)

◆ the piece should last two to three minutes, should start with a fanfare to gain attention and then a quiet passage for someone to announce the display before the dance section starts

You won't know how long the announcer will take, so build in flexibility here: perhaps a 'repeat until ready' section.

◆ the piece is to be performed by members of the year 10 GCSE group: two trumpeters, two saxophonists, three flautists, two violinists (both good, but nervous about playing on their own), two keyboard players, an electric guitarist, and a bass guitar player. Choose five of these performers for your piece.

Find out what these performers can do well, especially those who are less experienced. Although you don't have a drummer available, you could use an amplified keyboard as a drum machine.

Composition 2

You can compose anything you like for your second composition, although it too must be written to a brief. The brief can be written by yourself or can be suggested by your teacher. There are various suggestions for starting points for composing throughout this book: any of these could be adapted as briefs for your composition 2.

Unlike composition 1, it is acceptable for your composition 2 brief to change as you work on the piece although you will need to revise your brief to reflect your change in intention. You might start by composing a piece of film music but find later that the musical ideas that you have invented would work better as a lullaby for clarinets. Remember that your piece will be assessed on the extent to which it meets the demands of the brief.

Assessing your composition

To get a good mark for your compositions, you must take the following into account:

◆ Make good use of available resources. Try also to be imaginative with sound itself – don't compose your piece first and think about how you will set it out for instruments, voices or technology later. Can you use music technology effects, or the acoustics and layout of a performance space to be inventive with sound? Try having two groups of instruments answering each other from different sides of a large hall, or use pan in a recording to sweep sounds from one stereo speaker to another.

◆ Organise your sounds carefully, and have an overall sense of musical balance, form and structure. It is not enough just to invent musical ideas – try to do something imaginative with them. Think about how you can use techniques that you have come across in the Areas of Study.

There are some suggestions on how to develop and explore musical ideas in the 'Next steps' section on page 27.

◆ Decide early on what style of music you want to compose, and what medium you intend to use. For example, you may have chosen to write a song in a popular style for yourself to sing, accompanied by piano, rhythm guitar, bass and drums. Having made this decision, you need to listen to similar pieces so that you can base your composing on the conventions of the style and create appropriate musical textures.

✦ Make sure that you are able to communicate your intentions to somebody else through your piece. If you produce a written score it should be clear and include detailed performance directions. It should be possible for other musicians to perform your piece from your score and for it to sound as you intended. Any recording that you submit should communicate the essence of your composition to a listener. If you produce an annotation (see page 31) instead of a score there should be enough detail to allow other musicians, using the recording as a guide, to be able to reproduce your music accurately.

✦ It is essential that your composition meets the demands of the brief. Make sure that the musical elements you use are appropriate for it. If you are trying to write a fanfare it is unlikely to be effective if you have slow, ballad-like musical ideas. Ask other people to read your brief and to tell you if they think your music fits (it would be particularly helpful to discuss this with the organisers of the special event).

✦ Try to make your piece musically interesting and satisfying. Make use of techniques, devices and forms from music that you have studied to say something in music **yourself**.

Starting points

Many composers find knowing where to begin hard. Writing a brief is a good first step because it forces you to think about exactly what you want to achieve. This is especially helpful when the purpose of the composition is clear, as in the special event piece.

For hundreds of years musicians have learned to compose by finding out how other composers have constructed their music and then developing their own approaches. Bach learned his trade by copying out other composers' music. Elgar wrote a piece modelled on Mozart's 40th symphony. Mozart was still studying Bach's composing techniques towards the end of his life. All of these composers had strong musical styles of their own, but also learned from other composers. In your GCSE course you too will look at different types of music, discovering techniques that composers have used and using some of these as starting points for your own compositions.

Sometimes the best musical ideas come by accident. This is why it is worth improvising with your instrument or voice.

The composer Danny Elfman came up with the idea for the 1989 *Batman* film theme while on an aeroplane – he had to go to the aircraft toilet to hum his ideas into a tape recorder before he forgot them.

You could try to improvise against drum rhythms or accompaniment patterns from a keyboard. Force yourself to record a well-shaped improvised piece in less than half an hour. This is a particularly useful technique if you take a long time to get started with composing. If things go wrong, try turning mistakes into your next musical idea. It is also worth improvising in a group. This is a good way in which to find out about the sounds and capabilities of different instruments and voices. You might discover an idea with potential for growth. If you do, write it down or record it before you forget.

Aim for striking, memorable musical ideas. You may well have to work at this. If you find the main musical idea of your piece sounds like somebody practising a scale or arpeggio, you might want to try changing a few notes, rhythms or chords to see if you can make it more interesting.

Refining a musical idea

Your initial idea for a fanfare may be:

Try harmonising the tune with different chords, and change one or more notes:

Now try changing the rhythm of the tune, adding extra notes and different chords:

Add further notes to the tune. Experiment with different accompaniment styles – here the chords are played on a Latin American clave rhythm. Try adding percussion and a change of time signature.

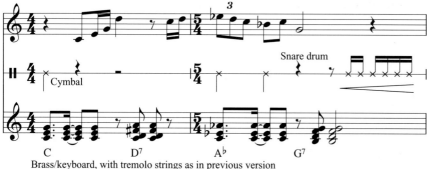

Brass/keyboard, with tremolo strings as in previous version

Next steps

You have studied some music, written a brief and come up with an initial musical idea. Where do you go now?

♦ **Repetition.** Bringing back ideas later on in the piece helps to give a sense of shape. Be careful about too much repetition though, as the piece may seem dull, while no repetition at all may make the piece sound bitty.

♦ **Adjusting the idea.** Try writing a variation of the original idea, or transpose it to a different set of pitches. You could also add or change chords, introduce another idea on top (a counter-melody), use different sounds (instruments, voices or music

Even Beethoven sometimes came up with fairly ordinary musical ideas and then had to chisel away at them, changing a note or rhythm at a time until the ordinary idea turned into something striking.

technology) or vary the texture of the idea by using more (or fewer) instruments or voices. Try changing the accompaniment, or playing the idea backwards or upside down. Other ways to adjust the original idea include: playing the idea faster or slower; adding extra notes to the end of a melody, or cutting some notes out; changing dynamics; altering the timbres that you use – try mutes, electronic effects (FX) and so on.

Be imaginative – what does a trumpet sound like if you put a duster up the bell?

+ **Moving on to a new idea.** Think about how different any new idea you choose to feature should be. It will need to contrast with your other ideas, but if it is completely different in style the piece may sound disjointed. Be careful about introducing too many new ideas, otherwise you may lose the sense of direction of the piece.

Form and structure

To judge if your compositions have a clear shape and a sense of purpose, you need to hear them performed. This way, you can hear if some sections are too long or too short, or if you use the same idea so many times that it becomes boring.

A piece in ternary form has the structure:

A (first idea)	B (new idea)	A (first idea again)

You will look at the way various pieces of music are structured on your GCSE Music course. It may help you to use some of these forms in your own music, but use them as a starting point and not as a jelly mould. If you are going to use a standard form such as ternary form, rondo (see page 59) or verse-chorus song form (see page 107) try to combine these structures with some of your own ideas. Most composers do not stick to the exact forms as defined in textbooks.

Try to have a picture of your piece as a whole. If you start at bar 1, then go on to bar 2, then bar 3 (and so on) you will find it difficult to gain this overview. One of the best composers for building satisfying musical forms was Beethoven. He would often place a tiny musical idea near the start of a piece. At first it doesn't seem to have any significance but later it becomes all important. Try to think about how each small musical idea fits in to the big picture.

Beginnings and endings are important, so think about the first thing the listeners will hear and how the piece will finish. It is sometimes helpful to compose the end of a piece first and then work out how to get to that point.

Trying out your work

When you listen to your piece, ask yourself questions such as:

+ Does it have the effect that you intended?

+ Is the balance wrong in places, meaning that the tune is not heard clearly?

+ Do some of your harmonies clash? Is that the desired effect?

+ Does the structure hold together convincingly?

+ Is there enough variety of texture and timbre?

Evaluating your work should be a natural part of composing. Your piece is likely to be much better if you listen to it regularly, thinking about what is or isn't working and making changes as you go along.

One of the best ways of appraising and refining a composition is to try it out in rehearsal. Ask your performers afterwards how they feel it worked. They will be able to point out difficulties and you can revise these passages as necessary. It is worth recording your piece at this stage to help you appraise and refine it.

Start your compositions early so that you have time to try them out and revise them in this way. Most importantly, try to complete each piece early enough to allow time to leave it alone for several days (or even weeks) and then come back to it with fresh ears.

Making clear judgements about your own work when you have only just finished composing it is hard to do.

The craft of composing

A large part of the craft of the composer consists of knowing how to create music that really suits particular instruments, technology and performers. Speak to performers and find out the practical range of each instrument. Discover what your friends find easy to play and what is difficult for their instrument/voice. Choosing an appropriate key can really help.

◆ Ask string players what pizzicato and tremolo sound like.

◆ Ask a trombone player to demonstrate a glissando.

◆ Ask an electric guitarist what their FX unit can do.

◆ Ask a pianist to hold down the sustaining pedal and ask a brass player to play into the inside of the piano.

It is probably best to compose for people in your music class, or in an ensemble in which you regularly perform. The vital thing is to make use of people who will be around for the entire time of the composing process and who will have time to try out several different drafts of your piece.

Imagine that you have decided to compose a waltz for a clarinet group in your school. Go to rehearsals and listen to other pieces for this particular group. Notice how vital it is to vary the textures in an ensemble. GCSE composers frequently forget this. The common weakness is to always assign the tune to the top part. Split the melodic ideas among as many parts as possible. Every one likes to play the tune. Use rests to break up the textures. Thick textures all the way through the piece can sound dull, so try:

Don't worry if the people that you want to compose for aren't very experienced as musicians. Just find out what they can do well and then make use of these strengths in your piece.

◆ full thick textures with everyone playing *but also*

◆ thin textures with only one or two instruments at a time

◆ high sounds answering low sounds in a call-and-response style

◆ having one instrument play the tune while the others play long held notes (or a drone)

◆ having instruments imitate each other.

Music technology

You can make use of music technology when you are composing:

◆ as a tool to enable you to hear what a group of live performers might sound like, using a sequencer and suitable sound sources

◆ to record tracks that will later be combined with live players/ singers

◆ to build-up a piece in layers using multi-track recording

◆ to originate purely electronic music

◆ to create printed scores of your composition.

It is not a requirement to use ICT but the GCSE listening exam is likely to include questions that require you to demonstrate an understanding of the impact of ICT on music. The more you use music technology as part of your course, the more easily you will be able to answer these questions.

If you compose a piece using music technology, get to know the capabilities of the technology. If you are using a computer sequencer, make full use of its features. A sequencer allows you to choose appropriate sounds, get the balance right between different parts, quantise notes so that rhythms are absolutely together, pan the sounds between left and right speakers and, in many cases, add effects (FX).

If you use music technology to compose a piece intended for live performers, make sure that you keep the live performers in mind throughout. Your synthesiser or computer soundcard can produce a sound like a trumpet, but it will probably not warn you that you have written notes that are too high for your trumpet-playing friend, or that you have demanded the impossible and asked a single trumpeter to play a chord. It won't remind you that your trumpet part has continued for several minutes without a single breathing point, nor will it tell you how long a rest you need for the player to fit a mute or turn a page.

Arrangements and samples

Ways to show your own creative input in an arrangement:

♦ combine your own musical ideas with the original material (eg, invent counter-melodies to go with a salsa tune)

♦ invent new harmonies

♦ create new textures for the music (eg don't copy the oom-pah-pah accompaniment of *The Blue Danube* waltz but devise your own accompaniment)

♦ invent new tunes to go on top of the chord sequence of the original piece

♦ change the style of the music (eg turn *Inspector Gadget* into a reggae piece)

♦ invent a new structure for the work, with your own introduction, ending and middle sections

♦ rethink the style of the accompaniment so that it really suits the instruments, voices or music technology for which you are producing the arrangement.

You have the option of producing an arrangement of an existing piece instead of an original composition. At first this may seem an easy alternative. But remember that you must hand in the printed music or recording that you used as the basis for your arrangement. This makes it possible to assess what *your* creative input has been. To do well an arrangement must show a large element of your own creativity. If all you do is rewrite the original piece for different musical forces you will not get good marks.

A word of warning about using material downloaded from the Internet. Compositions consisting entirely of samples of music by other people are treated as arrangements. The same advice applies if you make use of one of the many computer programs that contain pre-recorded samples designed to fit with each other. If you do base a piece on borrowed material, use the material creatively in combination with your own musical ideas and provide a full account of your input so it can be properly credited. Acknowledge any material used which is not your own, hand in copies of the original material (such as recordings of the individual samples used) with your composition and say where you found the borrowed material (eg a website address).

Group compositions

It is possible to submit a group composition for your coursework composing. You may well have done a lot of group composing at key stage 3 and this may seem like an attractive option. However at GCSE level individual work is normally expected.

If you submit a group composition you will only get credit for the parts where you can identify material that you individually created. If it is not clear exactly who composed what, no one will gain any marks.

We strongly advise you to avoid group compositions.

Presenting your work

You are *strongly* advised to record your piece as well as producing a score. Don't hand in a written score that you have been unable to try out with the intended musical forces: composing is not a paper exercise.

For each of your two compositions you will need to submit **either** a score, with a recording wherever possible, **or** a recording accompanied by a detailed annotation. You will also need to include a copy of your composing brief for each piece and to complete a *Candidate Record Form*.

Scores   Scores may be a full score in staff notation, a chord progression with lyrics, a chart like those in the jazz 'real books', guitar tablature or a lead sheet based on the melody-with-chords format employed in the 'busker's books'. If you choose a less-detailed type of notation remember to show how the sections of your piece (for example, verses and choruses) follow one another rather than simply type out the lyrics with chord symbols. If you use tablature you might make your intentions clearer if you also indicate rhythms. If you produce a graphic score, make sure that it includes detailed directions to the performers so that you can receive full credit for what they do. Any composition that is not in conventional staff notation *must* be recorded.

Computer-generated scores are acceptable but should be neatly formatted and edited so they are readable. Don't assume that music played into a computer sequencer will be automatically transformed into a perfect score. Musical playing is not precise and mechanical – note starts and note lengths often deviate fractionally from their expected positions in order to make the music expressive. The software will record *exactly* what you play. If the software is allowed to translate this literally into notation, the result may be as confused and unreadable as the top stave below (the first phrase of *Twinkle Twinkle Little Star*).

In general, computer sequencing software is most useful for composing and manipulating sounds. Specialist score-writing packages are probably easier to use if your main purpose is to produce a written score.

Fortunately sequencing software has tools to edit scores! In the lower stave *above*, the computer has been told to move all the notes to the nearest crotchet beat and to adjust their lengths to crotchets (or multiples of crotchets). This is called quantising and is just one of the types of editing you may need to do in order to produce an acceptable score. If you intend to use a computer to produce a printed score you will need to spend some time getting to know how the software works.

If you don't produce a score, you must submit a recording with a detailed annotation making clear what you were trying to achieve. An annotation could be a written description of the piece or a diagram (such as a track diagram) showing its important features. Whether you choose a written or diagrammatic format, be sure to include enough detailed information about the composition to help the examiner assess what you have done. It is in your interests to give your performers detailed instructions about how to play your piece. Use your score or annotation to make your instructions clear to the performers.

In your annotation you should include details of:

✦ Style ('This piece is in a drum 'n' bass style')

✦ Purpose ('This piece is designed as the main title theme for a western')

✦ Shape or structure ('the shape of the song is intro, verse, verse, chorus, verse, chorus, bridge, chorus, chorus')

Annotations

It is important to make it clear if, for example, you composed guitar and keyboard parts in full, or if you just gave the players chord charts from which they devised their own accompaniment patterns. Both approaches are acceptable, but you will gain more credit if you have been fully in control of all aspects of your piece.

- ◆ Melody and harmony ('I based the main tune around a pentatonic scale, and later on I made use of a repeated four-bar chord sequence: G–B♭–F–G')

- ◆ Keys used ('The piece starts and ends in C major, with a middle section in G major')

- ◆ Instrumentation and texture ('I used a trumpet with a mute to get a distant sound. String instruments play chords to accompany the trumpet. At the end the string instruments stop playing, leaving the trumpet playing a single melodic line')

- ◆ Dynamics ('The piece starts quietly before building up to a climax and then ending quietly')

- ◆ Musical devices used ('I used an ostinato pattern and a drone on the notes G and D throughout the first section')

- ◆ Music technology used ('I used a PC with Cubasis and a Tascam Portastudio with Alesis Microverb effects unit. I put some reverb on the voice part and used pan to place the two string instruments to left and right in the stereo mix')

- ◆ Special features ('There is a saxophone solo in the middle, performed by my friend. I worked out an improvisation using the blues scale and recorded it on tape for my friend to learn').

Recordings

Although the actual recording quality is not assessed for your coursework composing, getting a good recording will be satisfying for you and will help your piece to make a good impression.

Recordings may be on cassette tape or CD. If you make a live recording you should carry out a sound check and you may have to move microphones around so that everything can be heard clearly. Try to record more than one take. If you make a live recording with only one or two microphones, position your performers carefully so that the balance of the parts is right. Before you start recording, ask your performers to play as loudly as possible. This is so that you can set the recording level. If you set the recording level too low you will get poor sound (with lots of hiss if you are recording to tape). If you set the recording level too high you will get distortion. Bear in mind that performers may play even louder when they get carried away in the real performance.

Putting the finishing touches to a recording is important, as any record producer will tell you. Here are some suggestions to help you make better recordings:

- ◆ Record several versions and check them. Can you hear all the tracks/parts? Are any distorted? Is the recording balanced between left and right hand speakers?

- ◆ You can often use the equalisers (EQ) to reduce hiss or bring out an instrument.

- ◆ You can use the pan controls to place instruments in the left/right mix.

- ◆ Some instruments (especially vocals, pianos, drums and solos) often sound better if they are recorded with a little reverberation. Always record tracks without special effects and add them later.

- ◆ If you are using a computer timbre and it sounds a little thin, try copying the track and transposing the copy up or down an octave (or delaying it a fraction). This will thicken it a little. You can also try adding an effect such as chorus.

Candidate Record Form

You will need to complete a **Candidate Record** Form which will be given to you by your teacher. **On this form** you should:

◆ give details of your **composing brief for each** piece and how the resources used and **musical ideas relate** to it

◆ describe how you set **about composing**/recording the piece

◆ include details **of any computer** software or other music technology used

◆ make it clear **if any material has** been taken from an outside source (for example, samples, MIDI files or arrangement sources)

◆ give details of any help received from your teacher, a friend or any of your **performers**

◆ indicate which version best represents your intentions if for any reason your **recording** and score/annotation do not quite match up.

It may be that you have produced a detailed score but the recorded performance didn't go well. This is fine – indicate that the score shows your intentions best. On the other hand, perhaps you recorded your piece in layers, and only thought about writing it out later. You have made a good attempt at notating difficult rhythms, but you are not sure that you have got them exactly right. Indicate that your recording shows your intentions best.

Your composition

Ask for advice but don't necessarily take all of it. Some advice is factual and you would be silly not to take notice if your teacher or a friend (or the organiser of your special event) tells you that:

◆ you have written a flute part that is too low for the instrument

◆ you have used a difficult key for the guitar

◆ your piece is too long for the time slot at the special event

At other times advice is more a matter of opinion. You should always listen to what people say and think about it carefully, because they are trying to help you. If the advice is a matter of opinion and you feel strongly that what you have composed is really what you want, then stick with it. Only you can make final decisions about your composing – nobody can compose your piece for you.

Integrated Assignment

Dates

5 January: composing briefs are issued

5 May: hand recording and score/annotation to your teacher

5–15 May: examination

You may wonder why the word 'realisation' is used rather than 'recording' or 'performance'. This is because there are several different ways that you can approach the task.

The integrated assignment brings together all of the skills that you have developed in the different parts of the course. At the start of the spring term of the year in which you are taking your examination AQA will publish four briefs (detailed sets of instructions) for compositions. These briefs relate to four of the Areas of Study, and you will need to choose one of these. You will have to:

1. Compose a piece to meet the requirements of one of these briefs, and produce a score or annotation (see pages 30–32 for a discussion of these terms).

2. Produce a realisation of your piece in the form of a recording that is faithful to your score or annotation. This can be a recording of a live performance or one made using music technology.

3. Evaluate your composition (and its realisation) in a 30-minute written exam.

In essence the integrated assignment requires you to create music to order and to meet a strict deadline. You are also expected to show that you can compose music while thinking about the practicalities of how it will be realised. It is very important that you understand that this is not just a composing assignment: the realisation and the evaluation both carry as many marks as the actual composition.

You will have four months to work on the integrated assignment from the date that the briefs are issued, but you would be well-advised to try to complete a first draft of the composition as early as possible. This will leave you time to try out your piece, revise it and work on the recorded realisation.

Bear in mind that the spring term will be a busy and stressful time not only for yourself but also for any of your friends that you need to perform your piece. You will need to plan very carefully to make sure there is ample time to produce a really good recording of your piece. Do not leave everything to the last minute.

Composing briefs

You will have to choose one from a selection of four composing briefs. There will be one from each of these Areas of Study:

◆ Music for Film

◆ Music for Dance

◆ Orchestral Landmarks

◆ The Popular Song since 1960.

There will not be a brief from Music for Special Events, as you will compose a piece relating to this as part of your coursework composing (see page 24).

Each brief requires you to demonstrate your knowledge and understanding of the relevant Area of Study. Choosing the right brief is one of the most important decisions that you will have to make on the GCSE course. You should look carefully at each brief to decide which one you want to work with. Make sure that you fully understand what is required. It is okay to ask your teacher for advice at this stage. You might want to try starting more than one brief to see how things go, but if you do this, make sure that you make a final decision very quickly and then stick to it.

Starting on page 38 there are four sample Integrated Assignment briefs. These are obviously not the ones that you will have to work with for the real examination, but they should give you some idea of the sort of thing to expect, and you can use them for practice.

You will notice that each brief has a similar pattern – the real examination briefs will almost certainly use this same pattern.

Each brief:

♦ Links clearly to one of the Areas of Study.

♦ Contains a set of bullet points giving instructions for what your composition should contain. You should read these very carefully, as you will be assessed on the extent to which your piece meets these requirements.

♦ Gives suggestions for related listening. Try to listen to the listed music, as this should give you some ideas to get your own composition going.

Realisation

This task consists of making a realisation of your piece. You might (depending on the demands of the brief):

♦ Compose for yourself, perhaps with a group of friends, rehearse and then make a recording of a live performance. You could direct an ensemble if you don't wish to play or sing in the piece.

♦ Work in a recording studio with live musicians (or on your own) using a multitrack recorder to build up a recording in layers.

♦ Work alone on a piece composed for music technology resources, or that uses technology to realise a piece designed for live instruments. In this situation you may well be composing and realising the piece at one and the same time.

♦ Combine a music-technology backing with live performers recorded on top.

You have to show that you can control the transfer of your composition from a score (or your imagination) to a recording, and can use your initiative to solve any problems that might occur. This might involve organising and rehearsing performers, developing conducting skills or learning how to use the features of music technology to get an expressive recorded performance. You may well be composing for performers who are not very experienced, or using music technology that has limitations, so plan your piece with these restrictions in mind.

The session in which you record your piece can be one of the most challenging and rewarding parts of the GCSE Music course. If your piece is at all complicated it may take some time to get it together – remember that you know how it should sound, but your performers don't have this inside knowledge of the work. It is your responsibility to help them to understand the details and musical style of your piece so that you can produce an expressive recording that communicates what the music is about. All of this takes time: don't leave things until the last minute. Performers will need time to learn their parts. Don't assume that all of your musicians can read music – you may need to teach some of your performers to play or sing their part by ear. It can be helpful to make up rehearsal tapes for your friends to practise with in their own time.

If you don't write a piece solely for yourself to perform, it is probably worth composing for people that you know to be reliable, even if they may not be the strongest performers – you need

To get a good mark for your composition you will need to make sure that your piece fully meets the demands of your chosen brief, and demonstrate your understanding by making use of musical features from the relevant Area of Study in your piece. See the section on Coursework Composing (page 24) as this also applies to the Integrated Assignment.

Your realisation must be completed under the supervision of your teacher, so that they can authenticate it as your own work.

The recording may be made on cassette tape or CD.

Test things out early. There is no point waiting until the first run-through to discover that the violinists are not able to play their parts, or that the microphone leads are not long enough to move the microphones where you need them.

musicians who will work hard at your piece and not let you down. Make intelligent and imaginative use of the performers or technology that you have available.

It may be that you can't get all of the performers that you need, especially if you are composing for large forces. You can overcome such practical difficulties by using music technology to produce your realisation. You can use synthesised instruments instead of acoustic ones, or could combine some live performers with a computerised backing track. If you intend combining live music with technology try things out as early as possible so that you have time to solve any problems that arise.

Problems

You should aim to make the recorded realisation match your written score or annotation as closely as possible – if necessary alter the written version to reflect any changes made during the recording. If there are still differences between the written and recorded versions you should mention this in your evaluation.

What do you do if you feel that you have tried hard but the realisation doesn't do your piece justice? The key thing here is to make notes of places where you are unhappy and mention these in your evaluation (see *below*).

Think carefully about what problems might occur in the realisation. These could include poor tuning, mistakes of pitch or rhythm, misjudgement about instrument limitations, problems associated with sequencing (in a music-technology based performance), poor balance on a live recording, too much background noise and so on. If you can't avoid them, you can gain good marks in the evaluation by showing that you are aware of the problems and can describe how you tried to overcome them.

Evaluation

This consists of a 30-minute written exam held between 5 and 15 May in the year that you take the exam (in other words any time up to ten days after the deadline for handing in your score/annotation and recording). You will be able to take a copy of the original brief into the exam, plus your score/annotation and any other notes that you have made: you are strongly advised to keep a log of how you tackled the demands of the brief and any problems that you encountered (together with your solutions to these). The evaluation carries just as many marks as composing and realising – it is a chance for you to show that you genuinely understand what you have been doing.

It would be a good idea to make an extra copy of the recording of your composition before you hand it in, so that you can listen to it the night before your evaluation exam. If you do this the strengths and weaknesses of your realisation will be fresh in your mind, and you can make additional notes to help you answer the evaluation questions in the exam.

Practise evaluating your work. Try answering these three types of question in relation to your coursework compositions – give yourself 30 minutes in which to write your answers.

It is likely that you will be asked to assess your piece in three main ways. You can prepare for the evaluation by thinking carefully about how you would answer these questions:

1. How did you meet the demands of the brief?

You need to show that you are fully aware of all the challenges of the brief and how it relates to the Area of Study. For example: 'I used the standard verse–chorus structure for my song, and added reverb effects on the vocals as this is the case in most popular music recordings'. You can prepare for this by reading through the brief and making notes on how you set about meeting the requirements. Think about any ways in which listening to the suggested pieces helped you to form ideas, how you actually constructed the music and any changes and revisions you made (with reasons).

2. During the realisation of your composition you will have met a number of problems. Describe these problems and say how you tried to resolve them.

It is important to keep a log of things that go wrong and how they were put right. In some cases the result may have to be a compromise or it may be that something goes wrong and there is no time to solve the problem. What is important is that you demonstrate an awareness of the situation and appear to be in control. Make it clear what you wanted to achieve, and that you are aware of areas where your piece didn't work as well as you had hoped.

Be honest about the strengths and weaknesses of your work, making detailed reference to features of your composition and the realisation.

3. Describe how and why the final realised version of your composition is successful as a piece of music.

Here you can concentrate on the things that went right. Try to avoid saying the obvious like: 'It is successful because it follows the brief'. Instead think about it from the point of view of the listener or performer and remember that a realisation is never the last word but just one way in which the piece could be performed. Think about other treatments. Could they have been better? Then try evaluating it from the point of view of the listener and performer. You might ask: Is it satisfying to listen to? Does it have a pleasing shape? If you chose the film-music brief, would your piece affect the audience's emotions? How? If your piece is dance music, would it be likely to get people onto their feet in a club? How? Are the parts appropriate for the instruments? Are the instruments used to their best effect?

Make use of musical terms, especially those that are directly related to the Area of Study.

You won't get the real assignment briefs until quite late in the GCSE course, but there are ways in which you can prepare yourself for this challenge at an earlier stage:

Preparation

◆ Listen to lots of music related to the Areas of Study, and practice composing pieces that link to the music you have listened to. There are several suggestions for starting points for composing related to the Areas of Study throughout this book. You may find that a piece you start in this way turns into your second coursework composition.

◆ Try doing dummy runs for the Integrated Assignment using one of the sample briefs printed on pages 38–41, then practice evaluating your work using the questions that follow each brief.

Prepare for the evaluation by making notes throughout the composing and realisation process, so that you will be able to remember all the problems that arose and how you tried to solve them.

Sample Integrated Assignment briefs

Your piece can be in any style. The pieces mentioned are only suggestions to get you going on your own piece. You can compose for any forces – you do not have to compose for an orchestra.

Sample brief: Orchestral Landmarks

Brief to be issued in early January of exam year.

Several orchestral composers have written music inspired by night time. Mendelssohn's 'Nocturne' from *A Midsummer Night's Dream* and the third movement from Bartók's *Concerto for Orchestra* show two very different examples of this.

Compose a piece, in any style, based around the idea of night. Your piece should last no longer than three to four minutes and should:

✦ have a calm, peaceful first section

✦ have a more disturbed section to interrupt the mood – perhaps like a nightmare

✦ return to the calm opening music, but now mixed up with some of the musical ideas from the disturbed middle section

✦ make use of unusual instrumental, vocal or ICT effects to create an eerie mood.

Suggestions for related listening

Mendelssohn: 'Nocturne' from *A Midsummer Night's Dream*

Bartók: *Concerto for Orchestra* (third movement)

Debussy: *Clair de lune*.

Britten: 'Dirge' from *Serenade for Tenor, Horn and Strings*

In essence the brief is asking you to write a piece in ternary (ABA) form (see page 28) but to make it more interesting by combining elements of your two main musical ideas in the final section.

The Mendelssohn is very calm and relaxed at the start and might give you some ideas for your first section. The Bartók movement is dark and disturbed. Listen to the opening – this should give you some ideas for creating an eerie mood.

A set of bullet points giving detailed instructions for what your composition should contain. You will be assessed on the extent to which your piece meets these requirements.

Sample evaluation sheet: Orchestral Landmarks

Taken in early May of the exam year.

The assignment asked you to compose a piece of music inspired by night. Now answer **all** of the following points:

✦ Describe how you created the calm mood at the start.

✦ Describe how you created the disturbed mood for the middle section – which parts of this music did you later combine with the calm music.

✦ Explain how you created the unusual instrumental, vocal or ICT effects that you used.

✦ During the realisation of your composition you will have met a number of problems. Describe these problems and explain how you tried to resolve them.

✦ Describe how and why the final realised version of your composition is successful as a piece of music.

The first three questions ask you to evaluate how you have met the demands of the brief. You won't know exactly what these questions will be until you see the exam paper, but you can prepare by looking at the brief and asking yourself how you set about meeting its demands.

The last two questions are likely to appear on every evaluation exam paper.

Work out where you want the music to coincide exactly with the action (known as sync points). It might help to write out a blank score or diagram so you can plot music against action. Your score or annotation should show these sync points, perhaps with some written notes identifying the relationship between your music and the pictures.

You should practise thinking how you would answer these types of question while you are working on the brief, and make notes.

Sample brief: Music for Film

Brief to be issued in early January of exam year.

Compose music for this opening sequence from a science-fiction film.

1. A dark, dense forest. Night time. The camera zooms in on a very small tent in the middle of a clearing. Inside a man is sleeping. From the forest comes a cry like that of a wild animal – the man wakes up.

2. The man comes out of the tent and looks around the moonlit clearing. He has the sense that something is watching him from the shadows. He picks up his rifle and moves cautiously into the forest. Something is stalking him! Suddenly a shadow rises in front of him.

3. The man turns and runs, a look of panic on his face. Behind him bushes are flattened as something gigantic chases him.

4. The man reaches the clearing and stumbles. In desperation he turns to face the thing that is chasing him and raises his rifle – but there is nothing there. Has he managed to lose it? His eyes search the clearing, but he can see nothing. He breathes a sigh of relief. A shadow covers the moon. He looks up – an expression of absolute terror comes over his face as something enormous descends on him from above. He screams.

5. The title sequence for the film appears: *The Creature!*

Your music for this scene should last no more than 3½ minutes and should:

✦ follow the complete story line and make it more dramatic

✦ have a memorable theme to represent the creature – let this theme grow during the sequence, so that it is only heard in its complete form when the title sequence appears

✦ create a sense of tension in the opening scenes

✦ build to a dramatic climax at the end of the sequence.

Suggestions for related listening

✦ John Williams' scores to *Jurassic Park, Jaws* and *ET*

✦ Max Steiner's score to *King Kong*

✦ Franz Waxman's score to *The Bride of Frankenstein*

✦ Jerry Goldsmith's score to *The Mummy*

✦ Alan Silvestri's score to *The Mummy Returns*.

Following every detail of the story too closely would be too busy for a feature film. Think of a simple mood for each section and try to depict that.

The title sequences to *King Kong, The Bride of Frankenstein* and *Jaws* create appropriate dramatic moods and have memorable musical ideas for the monster. *The Mummy Returns* has some good chase music (eg the bus sequence). *ET* starts with an effective musical scene representing a forest at night. There are tense musical sequences where characters are stalked by monsters in *The Mummy* and *Jurassic Park* (eg the kitchen scene).

Sample evaluation sheet: Music for Film

Taken in early May of the exam year.

The assignment asked you to compose the music for a sequence from a science-fiction film. Now answer **all** of the following points:

✦ What sort of monster did you decide the creature was? Describe how you created the theme for it.

✦ How did you create the sense of tension at the start of the sequence?

✦ How did you create the dramatic climax at the end of the sequence?

✦ During the realisation of your composition you will have met a number of problems. Describe these problems and say how you tried to resolve them.

✦ Describe how and why the final realised version of your composition is successful as a piece of music.

Many electronic keyboards have latin and samba rhythms built in – try using these preset rhythms to get your ideas going. The chapter on Music for Dance contains important information about clave, and gives some examples of salsa and samba rhythms (see pages 62–63)

Sample brief: Music for Dance

Brief to be issued in early January of exam year.

Compose a piece of dance music using techniques and rhythms from either samba or salsa.

The music should:

- include parts for drums or other percussion instruments that make use of characteristic samba or salsa rhythms (these parts can be for live instruments or music technology)

- have a melody line that uses syncopated rhythms

- have a varied texture that makes use of call and response between a soloist and other instruments/voices

- use a selection of instrumental/vocal resources from at least two of these categories:

> brass
> woodwind
> keyboard
> strings
> guitar/bass
> vocals
> ICT.

Suggestions for related listening

Rough Guide CDs to Salsa, Salsa Dance and Samba

Gloria Estefan: *Mi Tierra*

Brazil Classics 2-O Samba (Luaka Bop)

Latin: The essential album

Brazil: The essential album

Call and response is an important feature of carnival samba. The full band, cued by rhythmic blasts on the samba whistle, answers rhythmic patterns played by a solo lead drummer. In salsa there is much use of call and response between a soloist (vocal or instrumental) and the chorus, or the rest of the band.

Carnival samba usually just includes drums and percussion, but there are other types of samba with a wider selection of instruments and voices (see the listening suggestions for examples). A salsa band might have drums/percussion, bass, guitar, piano, horns (brass, wind or string instruments) and vocals. However the brief gives you a lot of freedom in the forces for which you choose to compose.

Sample evaluation sheet: Music for Dance

Taken in early May of the exam year.

The assignment asked you to compose a piece of dance music using techniques and rhythms from either samba or salsa. Now answer **all** the following points.

- Describe how you used samba or salsa rhythms in your percussion parts.

- Describe how you have used call-and-response techniques to vary the texture in your piece.

- Explain the reasons for your choice of instruments and/or voices.

- During the realisation of your composition you will have met a number of problems. Describe these problems and say how you tried to resolve them.

- Describe how and why the final realised version of your composition is successful as a piece of music.

This is a subtle way to remind you to avoid bad language or offensive material in the lyrics.

You will need to work quite closely with the singer to arrive at a part that suits them (it can be difficult for a classically trained singer to do rock, or for a folk singer to do rap). If you are the singer, then compose around your interests and strengths – and keep in mind what sort of backing you want.

In essence you are asked to write for a four-piece band as a minimum. This is most likely to be singer, rhythm guitar, bass and drums. Of course, some backing vocals, a lead line and some strings could add important variety. Alternatively you could have any instruments that you like to work with the singer and drums.

This requires you to show your understanding of the Area of Study by using some aspect of world musics or music technology as part of your song. See the chapter on *The Popular Song since 1960* for ideas about how you might do this.

There needs to be some variety – perhaps by making a slight change of pattern or feel in the choruses (or middle section) or by using drum fills.

You should devote some time to writing an effective chorus – many verses are fairly simple and consist of words sung to a repeated note or two, but it is the chorus that makes the song.

Sample brief: The Popular Song since 1960

Brief to be issued in early January of exam year.

Compose a song based on **one** of these ideas: the need for people to live and work together in peace; loneliness; the stress of modern life (eg having to do GCSEs); finding or losing someone you love; you can do anything if you believe in yourself.

The music can be in any style and should:

✦ be suitable for broadcasting on national radio

✦ be appropriate for the subject matter of the words/lyrics

✦ **either** use some musical features or techniques from world musics **or** use music technology as an important part of the song

✦ contain the following elements:

  ✦ at least one solo voice (backing vocals using live voices or a multitracked voice may be used in addition)

  ✦ a live or synthesised drum track

  ✦ at least two instruments, which may be live or synthesised

  ✦ a memorable hook.

Suggestions for related listening

See the chapter on *Popular Song since 1960* (page 100) for suggestions that relate to the particular style of music on which you would like to base your song.

Sample evaluation sheet: The Popular Song since 1960

Taken in early May of the exam year.

The assignment asked you to compose a song on a given theme. Now answer **all** of the following points.

✦ Describe how your music is appropriate for the subject matter of the words/lyrics.

✦ Describe how you used **either** features or techniques from world musics **or** music technology in your song.

✦ Explain why you chose the particular musical elements and/or devices to create a memorable hook.

✦ During the realisation of your composition you will have met a number of problems. Describe these problems and say how you tried to resolve them.

✦ Describe how and why the final realised version of your composition is successful as a piece of music.

Music for Film

Many of the musical examples in this chapter have been simplified and/or **transposed** into easier keys. They should be taken as a general guide to the music being studied.

In the Listening and Appraising test there are likely to be questions that ask you to identify how composers have used musical features for specific dramatic effects, such as:

◆ creating a sense of time or place

◆ creating an appropriate mood

◆ depicting characters

◆ creating and releasing tension.

Film 57'; CD track 13 (1' 18") means that the music being discussed can be heard at 57 minutes into the film and one minute 18 seconds into track 13 on the CD. If you are using video, set the counter to zero at the moment the actual film starts – on DVD this happens automatically.

You can explore any appropriate film music as long as you study at least one film from each of three categories, western, fantasy and thriller. There are certain musical concepts that you will need to know and in this chapter we explore how these have been used dramatically in a selection of films. There are plenty of other good film scores that you could explore in this way. Try to get into the habit of listening carefully to the music in any film that you watch.

The western: landscapes and peoples of the Americas

The Magnificent Seven

The original soundtrack recording of *The Magnificent Seven* is available on MGM (RCD 10741). The start of the title music is in AQAA, page 8.

Elmer Bernstein's music for *The Magnificent Seven* (1960) is one of the classic western film scores. The story tells of a group of seven gunfighters helping a Mexican village that is being destroyed by bandits. The heroic quality of the story is immediately apparent in the title music.

Syncopated rhythms heard in brass and percussion:

At bar 16 a big sweeping string tune is heard over **syncopated** urgent rhythms from brass and percussion. All of the notes in the tune (and all of the harmonies, apart from one chord) come from the E♭-major scale. The simplicity of this bold, diatonic theme with its clearly differentiated accompaniment helps create the uplifting 'open-air' atmosphere.

Bernstein, *The Magnificent Seven*, main theme, bars 16–22

A chord of D♭-major appears in bar 22. This is a major chord on the flattened seventh degree of the scale. The seventh note of a E♭-major scale is D, but the D♭-major chord is built on D♭ – one semitone lower (or flatter) than the normal seventh note of the scale. Using this chord gives a hint of the mixolydian scale, which has a folk-like quality. This type of chord appears a lot in film music. You can hear it in the main theme of *Star Wars* (1977), composed by John Williams.

Like many westerns this is a simple story of good versus evil. Later in the film the music associated with Calvera and his bandits has a sinister quality that contrasts strongly with the optimistic feel of the *Magnificent Seven* theme. Both of these themes can be heard one after the other at the opening of the film (MGM CD track 1).

The Magnificent Seven, 'Calvera's Theme', opening

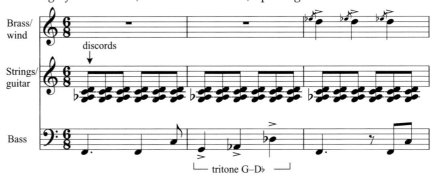

The key of 'Calvera's Theme' is far less obvious than it is in the main theme. There are no clear cadences, although all of the notes belong to different forms of the scale of F minor. Listen carefully and think about how contrasting musical elements have been used to create the mood. For example, in bars 2 and 3 the cross-rhythms arising from the use of three crotchets in bars of $\frac{6}{8}$ time create a Spanish flavour. Later in the film several other tunes have a Mexican/Spanish flavour, reflecting the setting.

Based loosely on history, *Pocahontas* (1995) tells the story of the love affair between the Englishman John Smith and the Native American Indian Pocahontas. This is set against a background of the conflict between English settlers arriving in America to cut down trees and search for gold, and the Native American Indians who have always lived there.

Don't be fooled into thinking that, because this is a Disney film, it only consists of songs for children. Alan Menken's Oscar-winning score is highly atmospheric: the overall effect is of a powerful piece of music theatre dealing with serious issues (the need for understanding between different cultures). There are plenty of songs, but they are very much part of the action: indeed the fusion of music and drama in this film is at a level that many operas fail to reach. Look for example at how the music, words and visuals come together in the song 'Colours of the Wind' – this is something that animation is able to do well.

The score makes full use of operatic conventions. An example of this is the climax of the film (the musical number 'Savages'). Here the Native Americans and the English settlers (who each see the other as savages) are heading for war while Pocahontas is caught in the middle trying to stop the fight. The music that she sings (taken from songs earlier in the film) contrasts strongly with the 'savages' music sung by the warriors. The whole scene builds up into a full-scale climax that is highly dramatic.

If you listen to the soundtrack or watch the film, you will quickly notice that the tunes of the songs get reused in the background music of other scenes. In other words they function as **leitmotifs**. As an example of this listen to the governor's song when he is gleefully ordering the American forests to be ripped up in the search for gold ('Mine, Mine, Mine', CD Track 9 (0' 26"); film just after 25'):

Governor Ratcliff

Backing: mainly strings (pizzicato bass) and flute

Later in the film, when the governor turns nasty, you hear a dark, sinister version of this tune ('Ratcliff's Plan', CD Track 21 (1' 31"); Film just after 51' 30"):

Slow and sinister

Backing: heavy brass, drum rolls

Pocahontas

The original soundtrack for *Pocahontas* is available from Warner (0927443662). The film is available on Walt Disney Home Video (D888350, DVD; D274522, VHS).

'Colours of the Wind', Warner CD track 11; film 37' 30"

'Savages', Warner CD track 13; film 64'.

In the 19th century the German composer Wagner used short musical motifs to represent characters or ideas (such as the hero, 'love' or 'fate'). These musical motifs come back in many different forms, reflecting the changing dramatic situation. He called these leitmotifs. Leitmotifs are common in film music, partly because several early-film composers (such as Eric Korngold) had previously written operas in the style of Wagner.

The way in which this tune has been transformed matches the change in the governor's mood – an excellent example of musical characterisation.

For your GCSE you need to show that you understand how composers use music to give a sense of time and place, and you are asked to study films that deal with the 'landscapes and peoples of the Americas'. *Pocahontas* is of course a Disney film and it would perhaps be unlikely to find genuine Native American music in such a film. Instead the composer has combined some American elements (such as the sound of the Native American flute and powwow drums) with his own style.

Pentatonic (five-note) scales are found in many folk cultures across the world, including Native American music. Many of the tunes in *Pocahontas* are based on pentatonic scales (see page 11) and this helps give the music a folk-like quality.

The song sung by the English settlers at the beginning of the film ('The Virginia Company') is also based on a pentatonic scale. This song links to a very different type of folk tradition: the sea shanty. Maybe the composer wanted to show that the two groups of people have more in common than they realise.

The melody of the verse section of 'Colours of the Wind' ('You think you own whatever land you land on') is also based on the pentatonic scale.

Pentatonic melodies in *Pocahontas*:

'Steady as the Beating Drum'

'The Virginia Company'

Other film music to study

Jerome Moross' music for *The Big Country* (1958). The main theme portrays another classic western landscape and uses the major chord on the flattened seventh degree of the scale.

Superman (1979). Listen to John Williams' music and note particularly the sequence where Clark Kent leaves his home in Smallville (37' into the film): what is the music telling you?

We will look at Morricone's film score for *The Good, the Bad and the Ugly* on page 54.

Finally, *The Mission* (1986) is set in South, not North, America in the 18th century. Ennio Morricone's music makes use of South-American and baroque church musical styles.

? **Test yourself**

1. What is a leitmotif?

    ....

2. Name the next note in this pentatonic scale: F – G – A – C – ......

Listen to the first 60 bars of the title music to *The Magnificent Seven* (AQAA, page 8) **four times**, as you answer questions 3–7.

3. Which of the following occurs throughout the first 11 bars?

    ground bass   pedal   sequence   imitation

4. The main theme is heard in bars 16–29. Choose **two** of the following words to describe the accompaniment of this theme.

    legato   staccato   syncopated   contrapuntal

5. At bar 30 this theme is repeated. What is the full name of the instrument marked 'Sn. Dr.' in the score that has an important part in this repeat? ....

6. At bar 46 the theme occurs again. What important feature of the accompaniment is heard but not shown in the score at this point? ....

7. What is the main difference between the version of the theme in bars 46–60 and the two previous versions of the theme?

....

Composing

Compose the title music for a western using *The Magnificent Seven* theme as a model. Try to use a flowing major-key theme on top of chords played in a rhythmically exciting manner. Try introducing a major chord on the flattened seventh degree of the key you are using.

Compose a piece of instrumental music for *Pocahontas*. Write for a solo instrument, using a pentatonic scale, and include a drum part. You could use either the major pentatonic scale (for example G–A–B–D–E), the minor pentatonic scale (for example G–B♭–C–D–F), or you could make up your own five-note scale. Alternatively, use a recorder (or any unusual pipe/flute) and write for whatever notes the instrument can play.

Compose a song for one of the characters from *Pocahontas* (perhaps an ordinary member of the English settlers or the Native American tribe, or one of the animals) in which they describe their feelings about the situation that they find themselves in. Then imagine that your character changes (maybe he/she becomes angry, or sad): try to alter your tune to reflect this change.

Classic monster/horror and science fiction/fantasy films

There are two film versions of *Planet of the Apes* (1968 and 2001), both with music that is highly effective in different ways. Both films tell the story of an astronaut who crash-lands on a planet in the distant future only to find that the pattern of evolution has been reversed: intelligent apes rule the planet, and humans are treated like dangerous animals and kept in cages.

Jerry Goldsmith's score for the 1968 *Planet of the Apes* was seen as ground-breaking in its time, and it still sounds modern over 30 years later. It was very important for the director of this film to make sure that the planet seemed truly alien – you will understand why if you've ever seen the shock ending. The music is highly **dissonant**, making much use of electronic effects (including **reverb** and **echo**) and unusual instruments such as electric harp, metal mixing bowls and a gong scraped with a wire brush. Listen to the sequence where the astronauts search the planet for any sign of life (film 21' 30"; Intrada CD track 'The Search Continues'). The music here is **atonal** (it avoids any sense of being in a key) and this combined with the unusual effects does create an alien feel:

Planet of the Apes

The original soundtrack for the 1968 version of Planet of the Apes is available from Intrada FMT 8006D. The 2001 original soundtrack CD is on Sony Classics (SK 89666). The 1968 film is available on DVD from Twentieth Century Fox (F1-SGB 01054) as is the 2001 version (F1-SGB 22080).

The extract in AQAA (page 17) is 'The Searchers' and occurs at 14' 47". Try comparing these two extracts.

gong scraped with wire brush

One sequence that stands out in this film is the section known as 'The Hunt' (film 30'). This is where the astronauts see humans being hunted through the long grass by figures on horseback. The music is violent, dissonant and full of **cross-rhythms** and **ostinato** patterns. Here is the first piano ostinato:

On top of this pattern are long-held notes, played on wind, brass or strings that crescendo into a 'snarl':

The 1968 hunt scene is analysed in more detail in **A Student's Guide to AS Music for the Edexcel Specification**, Bowman and Terry (*Rhinegold*), and the score appears in the **Edexcel New Anthology of Music** (*Peters Edition*). Try also comparing The Hunt with the previous two extracts.

On the DVD version of the film there is a good commentary by the composer that goes into detail about his working methods.

At the climax there is a close-up of the figures on horseback, and the audience realise that they are actually apes. At this point in the music a ram's horn and Tibetan horn are heard along with friction drums and squeaks from an electric bass clarinet. These unusual, raw sounds really help to bring out the shock moment of seeing the apes for the first time.

Danny Elfman's score for the 2001 *Planet of the Apes* demonstrates a different (and in some ways more conventional) approach that takes full advantage of advances in music technology.

Elfman describes his score as being dominated by brass and percussion and having a primitive, tribal quality. Most of the percussion consists of sounds that have been **sampled**. This means that the composer has recorded the sound of various percussion instruments and then stored them in such a way that they can be triggered through a computer. In order to get an unusual sound for the film many different instruments were sampled, and played in unusual ways (for example timpani played very gently with fingers, or played loudly enough to almost break the drum skins). These sampled percussion sounds, together with sounds produced by **synthesisers** were put together by the composer using software that can combine both **MIDI** and live sound.

The 2001 *Planet of the Apes* score is made up of a combination of sampled and synthesised sounds with a conventional full orchestra. At the recording sessions the orchestra recorded against 72 tracks of music that the composer had already put together on computer. You can hear this combination of live orchestral instruments and sampled/synthesised sound very clearly in the opening credits and in the 'Hunt' (15 minutes into the film). Sampled and synthesised parts make up more than half of the music heard in these sections. The DVD includes footage of the orchestral recording sessions ('Chimp Symphony') for the opening credits, plus a comparison of the 'Hunt' scenes from the two films.

If you have access to a computer sequencer (eg *Cubase* or *Logic*) you could try working in the same way.

John Williams' music for *Jaws* (1975) is one of the classic examples of leitmotif technique in film. In this story of a shark attack on a New England community the shark itself is not seen until over an hour into the film, but its presence is felt through the use of the well-known shark motif. This musical idea, based on ostinato patterns, is incredibly simple but highly effective:

Jaws

The original Soundtrack for *Jaws* is available on Decca 467045-2. The film is available on DVD (Universal UDR 90094) and video (Universal 0539583).

This semitone idea is used as a leitmotif, letting the audience know that something is there, even though they don't actually see it until much later. Watch the film: nobody tells you that this musical motif represents the shark, but as soon as the music starts up you know that it is unsafe to go into the water. The music (and your imagination) creates the fear rather than anything you see in the first part of the film.

The shark motif is heard at the following points in the film: The title sequence; 16'; 25'; 59'; 1 hr 18'; every few minutes from 1 hr 30' to the end.

Try playing the ostinato pattern (*above*) and then any of the following ideas that go above it:

These ideas are in different keys from the shark theme. Tension created by having two keys at once (known as bitonality) is one of the things that makes the music seem so menacing – and absolutely right for the film.

The composer uses the shark leitmotif to manipulate the audience's emotions. It is not heard in the false alarm sequence (where two boys cause chaos with a model shark fin: film 56'). Composer and director play fair with the audience here, but they also condition them into thinking that no music = no shark. Williams has described how,

The music accompanying the scene towards the end of the film where the shark cage is built (film 1 hr 46') is in the form of a short **fugue**. This is a clear example of the composer using a classical form for dramatic purposes.

Batman

Note that this film has a 15 certificate.

The CD of the orchestral score by Danny Elfman is available on Warner Bros 25977-2).

Batman theme based around these five notes:

The title music of *Batman* is in AQAA, page 23.

Superman theme 1

Superman theme 2

Most of the songs by Prince take place as source music within the film (in other words music that would be heard by the characters 'on screen'). This is sometimes called diegetic music.

having conditioned the audience to react in this way, later sections of the film deliberately create shock moments by having the shark suddenly rise out of the sea with no musical warning. Watch the scenes at 1 hr 17' and 1 hr 34': these really make you jump.

At the climax of the film (1 hr 54') the hero is trapped on the sinking boat with the shark circling. The shark is about to get blown up and as if to flag up this happy ending an optimistic major-key theme is played on top of the shark motif (see *left*). The optimistic theme in a major key is used over the end credits of the film: the music here washes away the horror, releases the tension and sends the audience away happy.

Danny Elfman's score for *Batman* (1989) is dark, brooding and ominous. It perfectly matches the film's vision of a nightmare American city ruled by crime. The script, music and set design all work together to create a dark, gothic feel to this film.

The 'Batman' theme is first heard during the title sequence, as the camera roams through dark alleyways that are gradually seen from above to form the bat symbol. The theme is based on a five-note idea that appears in new forms throughout the film. Listen to the title sequence and try to spot how many different ways this five-note idea is used.

Batman is seen as a troubled character, driven to fight crime after having seen his parents murdered. The Batman theme reflects this character and the dark setting. Compare this with John Williams' theme for *Superman the Movie* (1979). Superman is a much more straightforward, heroic character, and the contrast between the music for the two super-heroes is striking:

Batman (music by Danny Elfman)	Superman (music by John Williams)
Main theme (the five-note idea) keeps changing shape, reflecting the hero who lives in the shadows	Instantly memorable, heroic and optimistic fanfare-like main theme: the American feel-good factor
Largely minor keys	Major keys
Chromatic notes	Mainly diatonic based around tonic and dominant notes
Several rapid key changes, giving a restless feel	Stays in the same key for long periods, giving a sense of stability
Use of dark, low orchestral sounds	Bright orchestral sounds, led by high trumpets
Brutal military-style march rhythms	Accompanying rhythmic brass chords give a joyful kick to the tune

The villain in *Batman* is the Joker, and he is characterised by three different types of music:

✦ Songs by the pop star Prince, often heard playing from a ghetto blaster as part of the action (for example the scene in the museum where the Joker improves the paintings: film 59')

✦ 'Beautiful Dreamer' (a 19th-century popular song) that is linked to the Joker's obsession for Batman's girlfriend Vicky Vale (for example when the Joker visits her apartment: film 1 hour 18'). This tune can also be heard on CD track 9: 1' 30"

✦ A big orchestral waltz, first heard when we see the Joker

properly for the first time as he kills his former boss (film 36';
CD track 4, 2' 30"). This waltz also forms part of a climax in
Gotham Cathedral, as Batman fights for his life while the Joker
waltzes with Vicky (film 1 hr 46'; CD track 18).

Each of these musical styles is a deliberate contrast with the overall
dark musical feel of the film. Just as the Joker's white face, green
hair and colourful clothes are totally different to the grey of the rest
of Gotham City, so his upbeat tunes set him apart musically. Some
of his music seems insanely cheerful: a very effective way of
showing a disturbed, dangerous character.

The movie version of *Spider-Man* (2002) also has music by Danny
Elfman. Listen to the music for this film, and write down the ways
in which it characterises Spider-Man.

John Williams' score for *Harry Potter and the Philosopher's Stone*
(2001) is highly successful at capturing the magical feel of this film
about a schoolboy wizard. Listen to the CD and make notes on the
ways the composer has used musical elements to match the
different dramatic situations and moods. Compare 'Platform 9¾',
'The Quidditch Match' and 'The Chess Game', for example.

The *Star Wars* films (1977–2002 and beyond) span 25 years and
make much use of a network of connecting themes for the major
characters and ideas. Listen to John Williams' score for *Star Wars
Episode 2* and try to identify how many musical references there
are to themes from the earlier films.

Howard Shore's score for *Lord of the Rings* (2001) is dark and dramatic: listen to the writing for choir at the start. Several of the tunes
have a modal quality (for example the start of track 13 on the CD,
'The bridge of Khazad Dum') that fits the myth-inspired story, and
there are folk-inspired songs by Enya. Compare this score with
John Williams' score for *Harry Potter*: both are fantasy films, but
Lord of the Rings is much darker.

Composing

Danny Elfman says that his initial starting point when writing the
score for *Planet of the Apes* was the idea of ape marches. Try writing
your own ape march, perhaps using Elfman's idea of mixing live
and synthesised sounds. Use a computer or electronic keyboard to
put together a percussion-based backing, record it, and then invent
some parts for members of your GCSE group to play over the top
(perhaps while listening to your backing track through headphones). To give you some ideas, watch the way that the apes move
in the battle scenes near the end of the 2001 film (1 hr 26').

Compose music to the hunt sequence in either of the two *Planet of
the Apes* films. In the 1968 film this occurs at 30 minutes and in the
2001 version at 15 minutes. Turn the sound down and make a note
of the key features of each sequence and then compose music that
tries to give the overall feel of the action as well as making a special
point of some key moments. Try using Jerry Goldsmith's ideas of
ostinato patterns with dissonant ideas on top.

Compose a musical theme for a monster (eg King Kong, Godzilla,

Other fantasy films

Harry Potter is available on Warner Home
Video, D001013 (DVD), S021090 (VHS)
and on Warner Bros/Nonesuch/Atlantic,
7567-93086-2 (CD).

In almost the final scene of *Star Wars Episode 2* a massive army of clones is seen.
These are the good guys. So why has Williams accompanied the scene with the
evil 'Imperial March' music? Does this tell
us something about developments in *Episode 3*?

Frankenstein, Dracula, a dinosaur or giant snake). Think about how the monster would move, and maybe experiment with bitonality to give a scary effect.

Choose a superhero to compose a theme for. What sort of character does the superhero have? How can you show this in music? Now write a contrasting theme to represent a villain. Can you think of ways to combine the two themes for a final struggle in which the superhero eventually overcomes their enemy?

Test yourself

1. How is music used to characterise the Joker in the film *Batman*?

   ....

   ....

   ....

2. What is bitonality? ....

   ....

Thriller/Spy Films

The Firm

Note that this film has a 15 certificate, and is available on Paramount, PHE 8033 (DVD), BRP 0138 (VHS) and Rhino, 8122758742 (CD).

piano

based around blues scale

The Firm (1993) is a thriller set in a law firm in Memphis, USA. The hero is a young lawyer who gradually realises that the firm is a front for the Mafia and spends the rest of the film trying to escape from its clutches. Dave Grusin's score, written almost entirely for solo piano, is rooted in jazz and blues styles and seems a perfect match for the big-city settings.

The main title music for this film immediately sets the mood with driving **pedal notes** in the bass, **syncopation**, and use of **blue notes** (see *left*).

Towards the end of the film (around two hours in) there is a big chase scene, including the 'Mud Island Chase'. As well as playing the piano normally, the pianist uses the inside of the instrument to produce percussive and **glissando** effects. The overall effect is aggressive and dramatic.

James Bond

One of the jobs of the film composer is to create the right atmosphere or mood, and few scores do this more immediately than those of the James Bond films. The earliest of these films dates back 40 years and the distinctive 'Bond sound' was created in the early Bond films by composer John Barry. His James Bond theme is used as a signature tune throughout the series of films – even in those with scores by other composers. It is basically very simple, consisting of:

A tune on electric guitar:

A chromatic four-note ostinato pattern and pedal notes in the bass:

It is also unusual in that it contrasts the 'straight' rhythms above with those 'swung' in jazz style in the middle section: listen out for how the drum part changes at this point:

The James Bond sound also comes from the use of certain jazz chords that have become classic 'Bond' chords. These tend to be **minor** chords with added notes (see *right*). Try playing one of these chords on keyboard: the mood of the Bond films is created instantly.

A minor chord with added major 6th and added 9th   D minor with major 7th

Goldfinger

John Barry's score to *Goldfinger* was the model for many later films. Listen first to the title track sung by Shirley Bassey. This starts with a striking leitmotif (see *right*) followed by the main *Goldfinger* theme (see *below right*). The original James Bond theme is woven into the song and almost takes over at the end.

Much of the rest of the score for this film consists of variations on the musical ideas heard in this title song. Listen to the song several times and then watch the film. Listen out for how ideas from the song are used. The attack on Fort Knox for example (1 hr 24') makes much use of ostinato, with parts of the *Goldfinger* tune and leitmotif mixed with a military snare-drum rhythm.

Goldfinger theme

The film has another example of a leitmotif, for the villain Oddjob (see *right*). Watch the sequence (film 15') where Bond is knocked out while looking for champagne in the fridge. As we see Oddjob's shadow, the orchestra plays music for glockenspiel and strings based around one of the classic Bond chords.

Goldfinger is available on DVD (MGM 16178DVD) and VHS (MGM 161785). The music for the Raid on Fort Knox is in AQAA, page 25.

Oddjob's theme

Dm(maj⁷)

This music keeps coming back at points in the film where Oddjob is prominent, for example:

◆ when he is first seen at the golf club (film just after 24') and, later, in America (film 59')

◆ when he uses his lethal metal-rimmed bowler hat to knock the head off a statue (film 31')

◆ at the climax in Fort Knox when he is on the receiving end of his own lethal bowler hat (film just after 1 hr 37').

In many ways the score to *Goldfinger* is very simple. The laser beam scene, about 50 minutes into the film, is based on simple ostinato patterns, but is highly effective dramatically (see *below*). In this scene Bond is strapped to a table with a laser beam moving ever closer to him while he desperately tries to convince Goldfinger to keep him alive. John Barry uses only one chord in this scene.

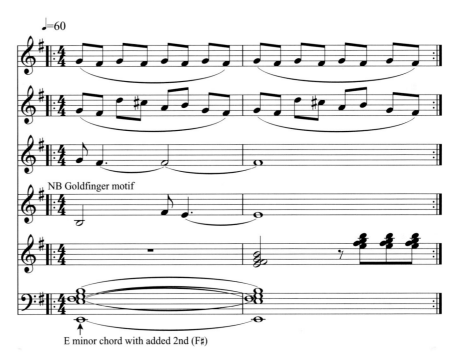

E minor chord with added 2nd (F#)

Try performing this with other members of your GCSE group, with the film going on in the background with the sound turned down. You should start with one line of the score and gradually bring in the others as the scene progresses. To make the music as dramatic as possible you will need to make decisions about:

◆ how to allocate the instruments you have in your group to different staves in the score – be creative with whatever you have available

◆ when to bring in the different instruments

◆ what dynamics to use

◆ adding ideas of your own to this texture.

If you want an extra challenge, watch the scene with a stopwatch and write down the exact time when key events happen. If you then perform the music at exactly 60 crotchet beats per minute, one beat of music will last exactly one second. You can then work out mathematically at what bar and beat a particular dramatic moment will come, and so decide exactly when to bring in the different lines of music. Set a sequencer to produce a click at this speed and choose a conductor who will wear headphones and conduct exactly in time with the click. If you have enough headphone splitters, you could all wear headphones to listen to the click. You will often see professional musicians recording film scores against click tracks in this way.

Tomorrow Never Dies

There are two soundtrack CDs for *Tomorrow Never Dies*. One has the songs but only two-thirds of the score; the other has all of the score but no songs (Gold Circle GCE 0125-2). Both include the 'Backseat Driver' track. The songs are available on various James Bond compilation CDs. The film is available on DVD (15919CDVD) and VHS (MGM15919S).

David Arnold says that John Barry is a major influence on his music, and this is evident in his score for *Tomorrow Never Dies* (1997). Arnold's score makes use of drum loops and synthesisers but, although written 33 years after *Goldfinger*, the music is recognisably part of the same sequence of films. The James Bond theme is still evident, similar chords are used and, like *Goldfinger*, the score often feels like a variation on the title song. David Arnold's original title song was replaced by the version sung by Sheryl Crow near the start of the film. However you can hear the composer's original version (known as 'Surrender' and sung by k d lang) over the end credits of the film. The orchestral introduction and main theme from 'Surrender' can be heard clearly throughout the rest of the film (film: end of pre-credits sequence; CD: end of 'White Knight' track).

Watch the remote-control car chase in the film (film 57') or listen to the first two minutes of the 'Back-seat Driver' track on the CD. David Arnold worked on this scene with Alex Gifford of Propellerheads. This is a very effective mixture of traditional orchestral and modern dance styles and makes for an exciting sequence.

Bernard Herrmann's music for *Psycho* (1960) is one of the classic thriller/horror film scores. Hitchcock chose to film *Psycho* in black-and-white and Herrmann matches this by writing the score purely for string instruments. The result is one of the most tense and nerve-jangling film scores ever written. Listen to the shower scene, with its screeching dissonant violins.

Other thriller/spy films

Test yourself

Describe what is meant by each of the following terms:

Atonal ....

Ostinato ....

Pedal ....

Syncopation ....

Glissando ....

Composing

Watch the motorcycle chase (film 1 hr 15') in *Tomorrow Never Dies* with the sound turned down (or invent your own action sequence). Compose music for this scene combining live parts for other members of your GCSE group with a pre-recorded drum-and-bass backing.

Listen to any of the James Bond title songs and work out the shape of them (verse/chorus etc). Use this structure as a model to write a title song for a new James Bond film.

Listening tests: Film music

Listen **three times** to the first 36 bars of the excerpt from *The Good, the Bad and the Ugly* (AQAA, page 12). For this test you should follow the score as you listen.

1. Which of the following best describes the first 20 bars of music? (Ring your answer)

    major   minor   atonal   modal   pentatonic

2. Which **two** of the following devices or features occurs in the first 20 bars? (Ring your anwers)

    sequence   imitation   ostinato   pedal   scale   ritardando

3. What is another name for the tam-tam, heard in bars 12, 14, 16 and 18?

    ....

4. Which instruments enter with a glissando on the second page of the score?

    ....

5. State two reasons why bars 33–36 are a surprise.

    ....

    ....

6. This excerpt is from the title music to a western. How has the composer created a sense of a desolate, windswept desert in this music? What do you feel the snare drum part might represent in this extract?

    ....

    ....

    ....

    ....

    ....

    ....

    ....

7. In *Harry Potter and the Philosopher's Stone*, Prologue/Hedwig's Theme: extract 1 (Warner CD track 1 from start until 0' 36"):

    (a) What is the tonality of this extract? (Ring your answer)

         minor   major

         modal   minor with extra notes from the chromatic scale

    (b) Tick one box to indicate which shape best represents the opening melody.

    A ☐
    B ☐
    C ☐
    D ☐

(c) The tune is played on a celesta (an instrument like a glockenspiel played from a piano-style keyboard).

    (i)   What family of instruments accompanies this tune (after 20 seconds)? ....

    (ii) Describe the music they play.

    ....

    ....

(d) Describe **three** ways in which the tune from extract 1 is performed differently when it is heard again (Warner CD track 1 from 0' 36" until 1' 23")

    (i)   ....

    (ii)   ....

    (iii) ....

(e) Both extracts come from the start of the *Harry Potter* film. Describe how the composer has used music to create a magical atmosphere.

    ....

    ....

8.   In the first two minutes of 'Backseat Driver' (*Tomorrow Never Dies*):

    (a) How many beats to the bar are there in this music? Ring your answer.

        3   4   5   7

    (b) Describe **two** features of 1990s dance music that you hear on this track.

        ....

        ....

    (c) List **three** standard orchestral instruments that you hear.

        (i) ....

        (ii) ....

        (iii) ....

    (d) This track uses the 'Surrender' orchestral intro, the 'Surrender' verse theme and the James Bond theme (see *below*). In what order are these themes **first** heard in this track?

        (i) ....

        (ii) ....

        (iii) ....

Orchestral intro

Main theme: verse

James Bond theme

Music for dance

Dance is all about movement. This may be relatively spontaneous (as at a rave or a disco) or it may be carefully rehearsed, as in more formal types of dance. Formal dances include modern line-dance, folk dances, ballroom dances (such as the waltz) and historic dances like the minuet and gavotte. In addition, staged dancing – often in costume and with lighting effects – can be used to tell a story (as in ballet) or to enhance opera, musical shows and spectacular events such as the opening of the Olympic games.

The most important elements in any type of dance music are metre, tempo, rhythm and phrase structure since these all relate directly to the movements of the dancers. Let's begin by seeing what each of these four terms means.

Metre Metre is the way the underlying pulse of music is organised into repeating patterns of strong and weak beats. In dances such as the minuet and waltz the beats are in the pattern **strong**–weak–weak. This is called triple metre. The time signature $\frac{3}{4}$ indicates a triple metre of three crotchet beats per bar. Duple metre uses the pattern **strong**–weak. It can be indicated by time signatures such as $\frac{2}{4}$ (two crotchet beats per bar) and $\frac{2}{2}$ or ¢ (two minim beats per bar). Quadruple metre often sounds like two bars of duple metre stuck together, although you may sometimes hear the first of its four beats being given extra emphasis: **strong**–weak–firm–weak. It can be indicated by time signatures such as $\frac{4}{4}$ or **C**.

All of the time signatures mentioned above are known as 'simple' because they contain beats that divide into two equal halves when shorter notes are required. If the beats instead divide into three equal portions, the music is said to be in compound time. For instance $\frac{6}{8}$ indicates compound duple time – two dotted crotchet beats per bar, each of which can divide into three quavers. In very slow music you might count this as six quaver beats per bar rather than two ♩. beats. An example of compound triple time is $\frac{9}{8}$ (three ♩. beats per bar), while an example of compound quadruple time is $\frac{12}{8}$ (four ♩. beats per bar).

Simple triple

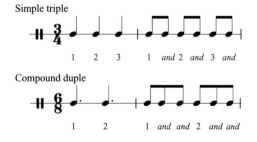

Compound duple

These two minuets are in AQAA, page 35.

This dance is in AQAA, page 32.

Look at the examples *left* and notice that $\frac{3}{4}$ and $\frac{6}{8}$ can both have six quavers in a bar. The crucial difference is that $\frac{3}{4}$ is simple triple time – three beats per bar, each of which can divide into two – while $\frac{6}{8}$ is compound duple time – two beats per bar, each of which can divide into three. Practise clapping these examples while counting the beats aloud.

Listen to the last two minuets in Handel's *Music for the Royal Fireworks*. As you do so, move in response to the simple triple metre of the music. For instance, you could slap your left thigh firmly on each downbeat (ie beat 1) and tap your right thigh lightly on the other two beats in each bar.

Now listen to the last movement of Bach's Orchestral Suite No. 3 in D. This dance is in compound duple metre ($\frac{6}{8}$ time). Once again move in response to the metre of the music, but this time notice that there are only two beats per bar, one strong and one weak.

Tempo is the speed of the beat and is another way in which one type of dance can differ from another. For instance the sarabande is, like the minuet, a dance in simple triple metre, but if you listen to the example from Bach's Orchestral Suite No. 2 in B minor you will hear that it is played at a much slower tempo than the minuet.

Rhythm refers to the organisation of long and short notes in music. Some dances are characterised by a particular rhythm that features prominently in the music. For instance, the tango is a dance which is often based on the rhythms shown at the foot of page 63.

Formal dancing usually involves set movements that are repeated in time to the music. The music itself therefore often consists of regular numbers of symmetrical phrases to which the dance steps can be fitted. Listen again to the minuets from Handel's *Fireworks Music* and make sure that you can hear how each one starts with a four-bar phrase which is answered by another phrase of the same length. This eight-bar section is repeated. The second half of each minuet similarly consists of a pair of four-bar phrases.

Symmetrical phrase lengths are maintained even in dances that start with an upbeat (known as an **anacrusis**). The gavotte is a dance in simple duple time that begins with an anacrusis. Listen to the gavottes from Bach's Orchestral Suite in D and notice how every phrase begins with this upbeat rhythmic figure. We still refer to the opening phrase as being a 'four-bar phrase' because it occupies the same number of beats as four full bars of music.

Tempo

This sarabande is in AQAA, page 28.

Rhythm

Phrase structure

These gavottes are in AQAA, page 29. Notice how bars are numbered when music starts with an anacrusis. Bar 1 is the first *complete* bar.

Although music and movement are closely related through the elements described above, it is important to realise that many of the pieces discussed in the first part of this chapter were not intended for actual dancing. Instead they were written to be played in concerts or in the home, where they could evoke the spirit of dance music for the passive listener.

The baroque suite

In the baroque period (*c*.1600–*c*.1750) the suite was a work based on a set of contrasting dances. These were unified by being in the same key, although the tonic minor was sometimes used for contrast, as in the second of Handel's minuets mentioned earlier.

Famous suites for orchestra from the late baroque period include Handel's *Water Music* and his *Music for the Royal Fireworks*, and Bach's four orchestral suites. These all begin with a long opening movement called an overture before the dances themselves. We will take a closer look at Bach's Orchestral Suite No. 3 in D on pages 85–86.

Baroque composers also wrote suites for solo instruments such as the harpsichord. You will find many different types of dance in both types of suite – here are some of the more common ones, with their main characteristics.

Baroque suites for keyboard include the six 'French Suites' and six 'English' Suites by J. S. Bach. Try to listen to some of the dances from these suites.

Gavotte

Listen again to the pair of gavottes by Bach in AQAA. What similarities and differences can you spot between them?

The gavotte is a fairly fast dance in simple duple metre (often notated with a minim beat – ie as $\frac{2}{2}$ or ¢). As we saw on page 57 each phrase usually begins with an anacrusis that occupies the second half of a bar. Most gavottes use melodic sequences and are based on simple rhythmic patterns with little or no syncopation.

Sarabande

Ornamentation in the sarabande in AQAA includes grace notes (printed in small type) and trills (marked *tr*). In the score you will also see numbers and symbols below the bass stave. This is called a figured bass and it indicates the harmonies to be played by the chordal instrument(s) in the continuo.

The sarabande is a slow and serious dance in simple triple metre (usually $\frac{3}{4}$ time). Sometimes the second beat of the bar was given special emphasis. The example in AQAA is from Bach's Orchestral Suite No. 2 in B minor (for flute, strings and continuo) and in this particular sarabande the serious style is underlined by a **canon** between the treble and bass parts. In all sarabandes the slow tempo encouraged the use of ornaments to decorate melodic lines. These could be written out, indicated by special symbols or improvised by the performer.

Gigue

Bach's Orchestral Suite No. 3 in D major ends with the gigue in AQAA.

The gigue is a fast dance in compound metre (often $\frac{6}{8}$ time). The term 'gigue' is French and the initial 'g' needs to be pronounced like the French 'je' – the dance should not be described as a 'gig'! However it is probably related to the jig, a dance found in British and Irish folk music. Baroque suites often end with a gigue.

Bourrée

The bourrée, like the gavotte, is in simple duple metre and is fairly fast in tempo. But there is an important difference between the two dances. Whereas the phrases in a gavotte start with an anacrusis on the last beat of a bar, those in a bourrée start with an anacrusis on the last half-beat of a bar. Here is the opening four-bar phrase of the bourrée in Handel's *Fireworks Music*.

This bourrée is not in AQAA, but music departments are likely to have a recording of the complete *Fireworks Music*.

four-bar phrase

Minuet

See AQAA, page 35

The minuet (*menuet* in French and *minuetto* in Italian) is an elegant dance in simple triple metre (usually $\frac{3}{4}$ time) that was performed at a moderate tempo. It was the only baroque dance that survived into the classical period (*c.*1750–*c.*1825).

There are many other types of baroque dance, each with its own particular style. However, despite this wide variety, most dances of the time have a number of features in common. Listen again to the two minuets from Handel's *Fireworks Music*. They contain five features found in many other baroque dances. Both minuets:

✦ are in **binary form** – a short musical structure of two sections, each usually marked by repeat signs – ‖: A :‖:B :‖

✦ consist of phrases of regular length

✦ contain clearly-defined cadences at the end of both sections (work out which cadences these are in Handel's two minuets)

✦ make prominent use of sequences, especially in the B sections (see how many you can spot)

✦ use a limited number of rhythm patterns to make the rhythmic character of the dance abundantly clear.

There are several other important features to notice in these two minuets. The *Music for the Royal Fireworks* was composed for a huge outdoor celebration. So that everyone could hear it Handel specified a vast orchestra but he wrote in a style that creates a grand effect through simplicity. In Minuet I the first phrase is based on just the tonic chord – and throughout the rest of the dance Handel used mainly primary triads (chords I, IV and V) in root position. Before the 19th century brass instruments did not have valves and were therefore limited in the number of different pitches they could play. By keeping to D major throughout the first minuet, and by using mainly primary triads, Handel is able to maximise his use of horns and trumpets. Much other baroque ceremonial music is in D major for this same reason – see the pieces discussed on pages 73–74.

Now listen to how the second minuet contrasts with the first:

◆ it is in the tonic minor (ie D minor instead of D major)

◆ the brass and timpani are silent

◆ it uses a thinner **texture**.

Minuet II consists of a three-part texture (two parts in the treble clef and one in the bass). This became known as a 'trio', and the name stuck as the term for a middle section, even if it used more than three parts. Many late 18th-century works include a 'minuet and trio' and in the 19th century the term trio was often used for the middle section of marches and polkas.

Both minuets include a rhythmic feature found before important cadences in many triple-time pieces of the baroque period. It is a type of **syncopation** called a **hemiola** and it gives a kick to the rhythm by creating the impression that two bars of $\frac{3}{4}$ time have become three bars of $\frac{2}{4}$. This is accomplished by the use of tied notes and careful positioning of chord changes. The example *right* shows the hemiola in Minuet II but you should have no difficulty in spotting the hemiola at a similar position in Minuet I.

At the end of Minuet II you will see the words 'Minuet I Da Capo'. This means repeat the first minuet 'from the head' (ie from the top). The effect is to create a musical sandwich: Minuet I – Minuet II – Minuet I. We could describe this as ternary form (or ABA).

Ternary form is extremely rare in a single baroque dance, but it often occurs when the first of a pair of dances of the same type is repeated after the second dance, as here. **Rondo** form (ABACA) was occasionally used for dances – for instance, the second movement of Bach's Orchestral Suite No. 2 is a Gavotte en rondeau.

Test yourself

1. What is an anacrusis? ....

2. State two ways in which a minuet differs from a gigue.

   ....

   ....

3. In which musical form are most baroque dances?

   ....

The orchestra for the first performance consisted of 24 oboes, 12 bassoons, a double bassoon, 9 horns, 9 trumpets and 9 timpani, plus side drums in the final minuet. Later Handel added parts for strings.

Notated:

Sounds like:

You can hear another example of paired dances in Bach's Orchestral Suite No. 3, in which the two gavottes are performed in the order Gavotte I – Gavotte II – Gavotte I.

19th-century dances

Waltz

Although the waltz, like the minuet, is usually in simple triple time, there is no direct connection between the two types of dance. The principal emphasis in the waltz is on the melody, the accompaniment is often purely supportive, and the tempo is much more flexible (sometimes with a feel of just one main beat per bar rather than three individual beats per bar). Some composers used the style of the waltz to write music purely for listening to, but many wrote waltzes as actual dance music – both for ordinary people (as did the Strauss family) or for professional ballet dancers (as did Tchaikovsky). Waltzes intended primarily for listening often use pauses and tempo rubato to disguise the constant triple metre. Waltzes for actual dancing are much more regular, using a variety of 16- or 32-bar sections to extend the dance into a piece several minutes long.

Tempo rubato refers to an expressive 'give and take' in the pulse, so that some notes and longer than expected while others are shorter to compensate.

The waltz kings were Johann Strauss the older (1804–1849) and his son Johann Strauss the younger (1825–1899). Their waltzes dominated European and American ballrooms from 1826. They reached a larger public by being published as piano solos and arrangements for violin and piano. This meant that ordinary people who possessed a piano could enjoy waltzes at home.

If you've seen *2001: A Space Odyssey* you will have heard *The Blue Danube*. It is the music for the docking of the space ship at the space station. A recording of *The Blue Danube* is available on Decca Eloquence (467413 2).

Perhaps the most famous set of waltzes of them all is *An der schönen, blauen Donau* (On the Beautiful Blue Danube) by Strauss the younger. There are five dances in this set, each with at least two memorable themes. But what is most astonishing is the variety of melodic invention Strauss achieves within the restraints imposed by fast simple-triple time (one dotted-minim beat per bar and about one bar per second). Example 2a comes from the first waltz of the set, and you will recognise its swaying on-beat rhythms. It is accompanied by simple tonic and dominant harmony articulated in the conventional *Um-cha-cha* crotchet rhythm of the waltz (but note that a good orchestra will play the first *cha* slightly before the second beat – a rhythmic effect that is too subtle to notate).

Example 2

(a) Waltz 1, first theme

(b) Waltz 5, first theme

Example 2b comes from the last waltz of the set. It is in the same key and metre as Example 2a, it has the same simple tonic-dominant *Um-cha-cha* accompaniment, and similar melodic repetition. Yet its effect is quite different. This is because of the prominent syncopated dotted crotchets that throw an accent on the second beat of bars 2, 3, 6 and 7. And instead of rising broken triads (x) it is based on falling 6ths (y).

The waltz even replaced the minuet in the symphony. One of the most famous examples of this occurs in Berlioz's *Symphonie fantastique* (1830). This is an example of **programme music**: here the artist has a dream of himself in a ballroom, glimpsing the woman with whom he is in love. Associated with the woman is a particular musical theme known as the *idée fixe*, a motif that returns obsessively throughout the piece.

In 1830 Chopin met the elder Strauss in Vienna and heard him playing waltzes on the piano. He wrote home: 'After each waltz they receive terrific applause … the public is so pleased that it goes mad with enthusiasm – it just shows how corrupt the taste of the Viennese is.' But the 20-year-old composer soon realised that in order to succeed he needed to please the upper classes in Viennese and Parisian salons – whether they had taste or not. And this is just what he did with his *Grande valse brillante* (Op. 18) which he completed two years after his encounter with Strauss senior. It is in fact a medley of seven waltz tunes (like Strauss's *Blue Danube* set) occupying more than 300 bars arranged like a patchwork quilt:

See AQAA, page 36. The strokes through the stems in bars 1–31 indicate a tremolo (rapid repetition of notes). The symbol in bar 2 (upper stave) indicates a repetition of the rhythm of the previous bar.

See bar 120 in AQAA. An *idée fixe* is a bit like a leitmotif: see page 43.

Grande valse brillante is available on BBC Music Legends/IMG Artists (BBCL 4057-Z).

It is obvious from the title, tempo mark (*Vivo*), and general style that the whole piece is meant to be played as fast as, or perhaps faster than, a Strauss waltz.

A	B	A	B	C	D	C	E	F	G	A	B	A	Coda

This is music for a virtuoso set on astonishing the elite in a sparkling salon with brilliant piano playing. Example 3 shows the last eight-bar phrase of one waltz tune – C in the diagram above – and part of the next – D (both transposed down a semitone from Chopin's keys of D♭ major and A♭ major).

Example 3

Despite chromatic decoration and gentle discords, the underlying harmony (shown by chord symbols) is simple. If you play the left-hand part of the first eight bars you will hear exactly the same *Um-cha-cha* accompaniment we noticed in the *Blue Danube* waltz. Now try playing the right-hand part. Did you come unstuck in bars 4–7? This complex syncopation cuts right across the left-hand part in an effect known as **cross-rhythm** (the left-hand accents coming on the first beat of the bar while the right-hand accents fall on the third beat).

For a very different style of waltz by Chopin, listen to his Valse Op. 34, No. 2 in the AQAA page 43.

Polka

See bars 15–16 in AQAA, page 47.

The polka is an energetic folk dance from Bohemia (now part of the Czech Republic in central Europe). It is in fast duple time and the basic dance steps (quick–quick–slow) are often reflected in a rhythm of three quavers followed by a quaver rest. The dance came to the ballroom in Prague in 1837, then spread rapidly throughout Europe, reaching New York and the whole of America some ten years later. The example in AQAA is the *Pizzicato Polka*, written as a collaboration between the brothers Josef and Johann Strauss the younger in 1870. Both composers used the polka as a vehicle for novelty effects (ranging from explosions, through thunder and lightning to popping champagne corks) and they often chose titles to reflect the modernity of their dances, such as the *Elektro-magnetische Polka* of 1852. In the *Pizzicato Polka* the novelty is the use of plucked strings throughout the dance.

The many pauses and changes of speed (mostly not notated) in the AQAA recording indicate that this performance is intended for listening rather than dancing (indeed, the piece features in the New Year's Day Concert from Vienna every year, which you can watch on television). You can hear a polka more clearly intended to be danced in Act 1 of the opera *The Bartered Bride*, written by the Czech composer Smetana in 1866.

The Bartered Bride is available on Naxos, 8 110098/9.

? Test yourself

1. What is meant by cross-rhythm? ....

2. What is tempo rubato? ....

3. In what type of dance music might you hear tempo rubato?

    ....

Dances of the Americas

Salsa

Salsa is Spanish for a hot sauce. The name of the dance implies it is exciting and 'spicy'.

Salsa is a dance-style from the Caribbean island of Cuba. Cuban musicians emigrating to the USA have made salsa an important element of the dance scene in Miami and New York.

The dance is marked by its sizzling, syncopated rhythms and energetic movements. Its origins lie in an earlier Cuban national dance-song called son. As with other Caribbean dances son is a mixture of African and European (in this case Spanish) musical influences. The guitar, prominent in son bands, was an import from Spain. The simple, diatonic chord structures of the dance are derived from Spanish folk music. The African influence can be heard in the percussion rhythms of son. Many of the percussion instruments used, including bongo drums, claves, güiro and maracas, developed from African instruments. Originally the bass line in the dance was played on a marimbula, an instrument modeled on the smaller African mbira, or thumb piano.

The marimbula is a large wooden box with a sound-hole cut into one side. Thin metal strips are fastened across the front of the hole and plucked to produce the notes of the bass line.

By 1950 son bands were larger. Trumpets, flutes, saxophones and piano had been added and the marimbula had been replaced by double bass. When Cuban musicians mixed son-style with the complex rhythms of another traditional dance, *rumba guaguancó*, salsa was born. Cuban dance music is structured around a crucial repeated rhythm called clave. This rhythm is often, but not always,

Clave is correctly pronounced 'clarvay', though you will hear references to the 'claves', a percussion instrument frequently pronounced as rhyming with 'caves'.

played on claves. Every other musical element is designed to fit around the clave pattern. Typically, it consists of five notes, spread out over two $\frac{4}{4}$ bars (see *right*)

Notice that there are three notes in bar 1 and two in bar 2. This arrangement of notes is called the 3:2 *son clave*. The pattern forms the basis of the rhythmic structure of salsa.

This order of the notes can be reversed, in which case it would be referred to as the 2:3 *son clave*.

The new son-rumba mix was not called salsa until the late 1960s. Many salsa musicians were strongly influenced by ideas from jazz. As a result, jazz instruments and performance styles were incorporated into salsa during the 1970s. Listen to *Cumbia pa' Colombia*, AQAA, page 58.

Samba

The samba is the national dance of Brazil. Its drums and complex percussion rhythms derive from west Africa while its syncopated harmonies are played on Portuguese guitars. Here is a typical syncopated pattern of chords:

Examples of salsa/rumba can be heard in the Puerto Rican dance sequences of *West Side Story* and *Saturday Night Fever*. It also forms the stylistic basis for 'Latino' artists like Gloria Estefan and Ricky Martin as well as the rhythmic patterning of much steel band writing and the music of funk bands like Jamiroquai.

The Portugese guitar looks and sounds very different from the Spanish guitar. It has two forms, the coimbra guitar and the smaller Lisbon guitar, the latter plays an important role in salsa music. The Portugese guitar sounds at written pitch, has 12 strings grouped in pairs and generally has a bright tone colour, whereas the Spanish guitar sounds an octave lower than written, has six strings and a more mellow tone-colour.

The dance has two main types, rural and urban. The rural type is performed by smaller bands and is usually more adventurous rhythmically. Urban sambas are often played by large bands using saxophones, trumpets and keyboards. **Call-and-response** vocal effects are also common.

The samba is usually in a major key. It is in $\frac{2}{4}$ or $\frac{4}{4}$ and is played with an emphasis on the second beat of the bar. There is a rhythm played on the *surdo*, a resonant, single-headed bass drum (see *right*). Other percussion instruments often used include the *pandeiro* (tambourine), *agogo* (double bell played with a thin wooden stick or metal bar) and *afoxé* (a gourd covered with a net of shells).

Here is a typical *surdo* rhythm:

Samba is often combined with ideas from other dances to create dance-fusions such as samba-rumba and samba-tango. The samba-cancao is a popular sung samba. The samba-salao (saloon-samba) is a type of samba played at public balls. Listen to *Swing de Campo Grande*, AQAA, page 54, and notice the distinctive guitar sound.

Tango

The tango is the best-known of Argentina's dances. The dance became popular throughout Argentina at the end of the 19th century. It soon spread to Europe where it became a craze. During the 1920s the tango was superseded in Europe by the foxtrot. However it remains to this day a popular exhibition dance throughout the world.

The foxtrot is a fast ballroom dance. An exhibition dance is one danced at competitions and other formal display events.

The tango is in $\frac{2}{4}$ or $\frac{4}{4}$ and is marked by a repeated rhythmic pattern. Instruments used included violin, piano and double bass. After about 1900 tango bands began using the bandoneon, combining this instrument with violin and piano. Listen to Piazolla's *Libertango* (AQAA, page 50) which features accordion and strings, along with a bass built upon pattern (c) shown *right*. During the first half of the 20th century many tangos were written for piano

The tango rhythmic-pattern can take several forms, including:

The bandoneon is a form of accordion.

Listen to the Gotan Project's 2001 *CD La revancha del tango* (XL XLCD148).

The tango in western classical music

solo. By contrast, large bands were formed which contained up to four bandoneons, violins, cello, double bass and piano. The continuing popularity of the tango in Argentina has resulted in a number of modern bands which fuse elements of tango with ideas from jazz, rock and electronic dance music. One such band is the Gotan Project.

Several western classical composers wrote their own tangos. Stravinsky included a tango in his *Histoire du soldat* of 1918. William Walton fused tango, pasodoble and English popular song in No. 6 of *Façade* (1921–1922).

Test yourself

1. On which Caribbean island did salsa originate?

   ....

2. Identify one of the African influences on the development of both salsa and samba.

   ....

3. What type of instrument is a bandoneon? ....

The dance and club scene

Club dance music is broadly defined by its percussive elements, $\frac{4}{4}$ time and strict dance tempo.

The development of the dance and club scene has caused a separation between live and recorded music. Popular dance numbers associated with house music are initially recordings. But these recordings are then altered by technology in a process during which the original performances are made less significant than the role of the DJ in the manipulation of the recordings.

Edits of dance tunes are designed for specific purposes. For example a radio edit is relatively short. On the other hand a longer dance edit of a tune is designed to allow time for a live DJ to mix before and after the main themes it contains.

Disco

Disco developed during the 1970s. The music, which needed to be designed for dance, contained the following elements:

✦ a strongly emphasised beat at a steady speed

✦ clear-cut rhythms which were maintained throughout the song

✦ a simple verse-and-chorus structure

✦ a memorable melody.

Another requirement was that songs should be longer than the three minutes of the then-standard single. This need was met by the development of the 12-inch single which enabled songs of ten or more minutes to be recorded.

The film *Saturday Night Fever*, starring John Travolta was part of the disco era. Songs from the film's soundtrack by the Bee Gees successfully demonstrate the elements listed above (see AQAA, page 61). The dance scenes on film are lively but, by comparison with today, more formal in terms of dance movements. Important disco performers were Donna Summer, Rose Royce and Chic.

Rap

In the early days of reggae in Jamaica (see page 102) the B-sides of singles were instrumental versions of songs over which a DJ could talk. This process was called toasting and was the forerunner of African-American rap. Rap emerged as an alternative to disco in American inner cities at the end of the 1970s. The musical backing for rap was borrowed from existing records. The DJ Grandmaster Flash used a drum machine to link two tracks on vinyl records on two turntables together. Another DJ, Grand Wizard Theodor, was among the first to use the technique of scratching. This involved manipulating a record under its stylus to create different effects.

A drum machine was also known as a beat box; hence early-rap fans were called 'beat boys'.

The themes of early rap songs were about issues such as drug-taking, as in *White Lines* by Grandmaster Flash. Later groups like Public Enemy used violent imagery to express strongly-held views on race and integration. NWA caused a storm in 1988 with the release of its first album *Straight outta Compton*. The album contained a rap about gangsters and one that was hostile towards the police. NWA was severely criticised by many in the USA: *Efil4zaggin* (1992) was banned for a time in Britain.

The Los Angeles rapper Ice T became famous at the end of the 1980s for his anti-female stance. His album *OG – The Original Gangster* became popular in 1991. Also from California is M C Hammer, whose first album *Let's get it Started* sold more than 1.5 million copies. More recently Snoopdogg (formerly Snoop Doggy Dog), So Solid Crew and Eminem have become leaders in the field of rap. In this male-dominated genre the success of the female rapper Missy Elliott is unusual.

A form of rap called hip hop emerged in New York during the 1970s. The term was used to define the music, dance and art of New York's Bronx district. The styles of dancing included break-dancing (spinning on the ground or floor) and dancing with robot-like movements. Much of the art associated with hip hop took the form of graffiti. During the 1980s hip-hop singles became popular on dance-floors world-wide.

Hip hop

Hip hop has influenced some jazz and soul musicians: Chaka Khan's single *I feel for you* included a hip-hop introduction from DJ Grandmaster Melle Mel.

Dance music and technology

Some important techniques and devices used in the recording and manipulation of dance music are defined below.

The vast majority of popular dance music comprises four-bar sections in $\frac{4}{4}$. A loop is a short section of a tune, perhaps an arpeggio or a vocal hook (short, repeated melodic line). You can then arrange these loops to create your tune, bringing in sections as you feel they are needed.

Looping

Usually each four-bar section will fit harmonically and rhythmically with all other loops. This means that it will be possible to use any combination of loops.

MIDI stands for Musical Instrument Digital Interface. It is a standard for connecting and remotely operating electronic musical instruments and related devices such as computers and effects units.

MIDI

When making a remix small extracts are taken from an existing

Remix

recording and electronically transformed into a new piece of music, usually in a different style. The borrowed elements are often distinctive, such as the hook line of a chorus or a bass riff. The rhythm section and instrumentation used often define the musical style into which a tune is remixed. Remixes may also involve a new chord structure or a borrowed rhythm pattern.

Sampler   A sampler is a device that records, manipulates and replays digital audio samples. These samples can be modified to create new sounds or to play back the original sounds in a different order.

Sequencer   A sequencer is a device that can be used to record, edit and replay performance instructions, such as MIDI-note on and off messages. These are used to control instruments such as synthesisers or samplers.

Popular dance music styles

House   The larger beach resorts in Spain and Greece have lively club scenes. Some of the songs played on the dance-floors are so popular that they become summer dance-hits. When the holiday-makers return to Britain they are reminded of their summer raves whenever they hear those popular tracks. The hallmark of this house music is the use of synthesised sound effects.

Techno   Techno originated in Detroit in the USA and became the most important dance-floor style of the early 1990s. It drew upon electronic influences from European bands such as Kraftwerk and Tangerine Dream. The music of these bands was loudly amplified. It was also slow-moving harmonically, used rock-based chord sequences, and often included sections based on a collage of sounds.

Jungle and Drum'n'bass   These two styles are very similar and are both usually in $\frac{4}{4}$ metre. Indeed the terms jungle and drum'n'bass are often used interchangeably. However the origins of the styles differ. Jungle came first, and it was a meeting between UK-born Jamaican ragga and white-English rave. Ragga was an extension of the reggae-derived DJ tradition. Rave was a style which involved all-night dancing to synth-lead tunes. Jungle music itself is frenetic, with ragga styles and MCs playing to a break-beat at very fast tempo (up to 160 beats per minute). An MC ('master of ceremonies') initiates call and response between the audience and the DJ playing the music.

Drum'n'bass is a jazz-influenced style, and the music generally seems more crafted and considered. Influences include funk, and there are many sub-divisions of the style including, for example, Latin-American influences.

Technology is central to creating jungle and drum'n'bass music. The two styles rely on sampling and sequencing. Vocal lines are often taken from other tunes, speeded up and laid on new drum sections. Individual drum hits from a loop are often rearranged to create new rhythms with other sounds. Shy FX is the jungle DJ who released the tune *Original Nuttah* in mid 1994. LTJ Bukem is a good example of a drum'n'bass DJ.

UK Garage   UK garage is a fusion of jungle, drum'n'bass and modern rhythm'n'blues. It uses the same sounds and instruments as jungle and drum'n'bass, but has the polished sound of rhythm 'n' blues.

The style relies heavily on vocal lines. These vocal lines are often chopped up and played back in syncopated rhythm. UK garage rhythms, in general, are syncopated, and they have the break-beat influence from jungle. A key difference between garage and house is that synths in garage are not usually as sustained as they are in house. Garage tunes are less dense in texture, as individual instrumental timbres are each only present for a short period of time.

Trance

An important development during the 2000s has been trance. Trance became popular on the Mediterranean summer rave scene. It has a similar rhythmic drive to house and shares many of its characteristics. Trance is DJ-led and is distinguished by its use of repetition and echoing, electronic effects. The repeated sequences are often slow-moving harmonically despite the fast beat which underlies them. The contrast between the fast beat and rhythms, and the repetition and echo effects, helps set up a trance-like state in clubbers. Ferry Corsten is well known for his trance mixes and remixes.

Many of Corsten's mixes are featured on the two-CD set *Trance Nation* (Ministry of Sound MOSCD34) which was released in 2002.

Ambient

Sampled and looped sounds, along with a vocoder (a type of speech synthesizer and processor) can be heard in *1969* by Boards of Canada (AQAA, page 66). This track comes from the album *Geogaddi*, released in February 2002, and is in a style of music often known as ambient.

Test yourself

Listen to *Night Fever* by the Bee Gees **five times** as you answer the following questions. You should follow the score on page 61 of AQAA as you listen.

1. The wah-wah guitar part is notated with a stroke through the stem of every quaver. How is this rhythm performed?

   ....

2. There are small circles over some notes on the drum stave. How does the sound of the hi-hat cymbal change on these notes?

   ....

3. Which later section of the song is based on the introduction?

   ....

4. In bar 16, what does the keyboard player do at the point where there is a diagonal line in the score?

   ....

5. State a way in which the middle section (starting at bar 27) differs from the other sections.

   ....

6. In verse 2 the violins play a sustained C in octaves from bar 5 to bar 12. What is the technical name for this feature of the music?

   ....

Composing

Your Composition 2 can be based on this Area of Study if you wish. Here are three very different ideas to help you get started.

1. Compose a minuet (or other baroque dance of your choice) to be used as the accompaniment for a formal dance in an 18th-century play. The dance should be in binary form with two eight-bar sections. If you are not too sure about using harmony you could use the following adaptation of the chord pattern used by Handel in his D-major minuet from the *Firework's Music*, in this way:

: I	I	I	I	I	V	I	V :	: I	IV	V	Ib	IV	V	V	I :

Reread the points at the foot of page 58 to remind yourself of the important features of a baroque dance.

2. Compose a waltz using some of the techniques discussed in this chapter. Remember that there is usually one chord per bar and the harmony is often simple. For example, the first waltz in *The Blue Danube* starts with this basic 16-bar chord pattern:

I	I	I	I	V⁷	V⁷	V⁷	V⁷	V⁷	V⁷	V⁷	V⁷	I	I	I	I

Waltzes or polkas tend to be in several sections, each one characterised by a new melody. The opening theme usually comes back at some stage so that the structure might be a rondo (ABACA), ternary form with an extended middle section (ABCDA), or a more complex 'patchwork quilt', as described on page 61.

Some dance styles are more suitable than others for composing at GCSE. Garage and trance, for example, require skilled vocal and deck performers to achieve a convincing result so unless you have a talented crew to help it might be safer to opt for something purely instrumental/ synthesised, or which you can assemble using samples (but remember to include details about the way you obtained them).

It is often best to begin with the chords. Arrange them into the *um-cha-cha* style of a waltz accompaniment and then compose a melody to fit. Once you are happy with your 16 bars, try extending the piece by adding a contrasting section in a different key. End by bringing back part or all of the opening section in the original key.

3. Compose a piece in one of the following styles:

    ✦ **Techno.** Base your piece on synthesised timbres and/or sampled material (perhaps vocal). Techno offers an opportunity to show your skill at looping, cutting and pasting and remixing ideas. Some techno groups use samples extensively, for example Prodigy, while others prefer to programme timbres and loop ostinati, for example Orbital.

    ✦ **Drum'n'bass.** Try to make use of the techniques described on page 66. Aim for interesting drum patterns: the bass drum part in drum'n'bass tends to be rhythmically complex.

    ✦ **Ambient.** 'Chill out' music – an opportunity to blend timbres and create a dreamy musical landscape using 'synth pads' and sampled choral effects.

Today's club music is often composed almost entirely on a computer using MIDI timbres and sampled sounds. Familiarise yourself with cutting and pasting techniques, editing and looping patterns, and mixing the tracks on screen. Don't just use patterns straight off a drum machine and don't just download material by other composers. Demonstrate that you are able to cut and trim your own samples and match them with original material in your composition.

Listening tests: Music for Dance

1. Listen to the third movement of Mozart's *Eine Kleine Nachtmusik*, **four times** as you answer the following questions. (Most schools will have a recording of this work.)

    (a) Using the given rhythm, complete the melody in bars 6–7:

    (b) Name or describe the cadence in bars 7–8. ....

    (c) State **two** ways in which the melody of bars 9–11 differs from the melody of bars 1–3.

    ....

    (d) What type of dance is this? ....

    (e) From which period do you think this music comes? ....

    (f) Underline the type of ensemble that plays this extract on the recording:

    symphony orchestra   wind band   string orchestra   brass trio   string quartet

2. Listen to the first 25 seconds *of Libertango* **three times** as you answer the following questions. The recording is included in AQAA but answer these questions without following the score.

    (a) Underline the description which best describes the texture of this extract:

    contrapuntal   two-part   three-part   four-part   monophonic

    (b) The melody is played by strings and which other type of instrument? ....

    (c) Describe the bass part of this extract as fully as you can. Try to use the following terms in your answer: dominant, pedal, chromatic, ostinato, syncopated.

    ....

    ....

    ....

    ....

    ....

    ....

Music for Special Events

Because composers have to earn a living, they depend on people paying them to write new works. Many large-scale musical works composed before the second half of the 18th century were commissioned for special events by monarchs, aristocrats and dignitaries of the church. These were the people who could afford the expense of a major performance and, because they were known as 'patrons', commissioning works of art in this way was called **patronage**. Even today you will find that a coronation, a royal wedding, or the opening of a major new building is often accompanied by the performance of a new piece of music specially written for the event.

Opera

Opera is a dramatic fusion of words, music, spectacle and sometimes dancing. The birth of opera in Italy at the beginning of the 17th century marked a clean break with the music of earlier centuries, and its new vocal and instrumental styles formed the foundations of 150 years of baroque music. The first fully fledged opera – *Euridice* (1600) by Jacopo Peri – would not have seen the light of day had it not been specifically commissioned for the magnificent celebrations staged in honour of the wedding of Maria de' Medici of Tuscany to Henry IV of France in Florence. The story tells how Orfeo (or, in English, Orpheus) braved hell to bring his beloved Euridice back to the land of the living. The original Greek myth had a tragic ending that would not have been appreciated at such a special event as the union of the two most powerful dynasties of the time. So the plot was changed and Pluto, the king of the underworld, relents, releases Euridice, and the happy couple return to earth amid general rejoicing. Example 1 shows Peri's setting of a lament sung by Orfeo.

Euridice

Peri's *Euridice* is available as a recording on Pavanne, ADW 73723.

Example 1 A phrase from one of Orfeo's recitatives in Peri's *Euridice* (1600)

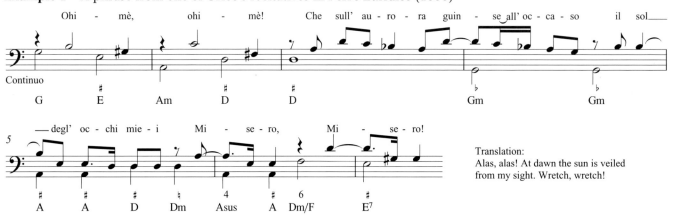

Translation:
Alas, alas! At dawn the sun is veiled from my sight. Wretch, wretch!

For more on continuo see page 73.

This is a **recitative**, a type of song in which the rhythm of the text is more important than flowing melody. In order not to distract attention from the words the accompaniment consists of the simplest possible bass part with chords improvised on instruments such as the harp, guitar, harpsichord or lute in accordance with the figuring (accidentals and figures under the notes). We have added guitar chord-symbols below the figuring to show the simple major and minor chords that are typical of early operatic recitative. But try singing the melody (an octave higher if necessary) and you will soon discover that it is anything but simple. This is partly because of Peri's determined effort to follow the rhythms of the Italian text, and partly because there are so many unusual melodic intervals. For instance, the interval between the C and F♯ in bar 2 is a **tritone** (three tones), a leap so difficult to sing that it was known as 'the devil in music' and strictly forbidden in medieval and renaissance music. Here Peri uses it to express Orfeo's anguish.

Oratorio

An **oratorio** is music with a sacred subject performed in concert by solo singers accompanied by an instrumental ensemble and often featuring vocal ensembles or choruses. In 1600, the same year that Peri's *Euridice* was premiered in Florence, a lavish work called *The Representation of the Soul and Body* by Emilio de' Cavalieri was produced in the Oratorio del Crocifisso in Rome. The 'oratory' itself was originally a hall, often built next to a large church, which was small enough to allow sermons and sacred music to be heard clearly. It is for this reason that Cavalieri's *Representation* is regarded as the first oratorio, but it would never have been written at all had the Oratorians not commissioned it as a special work designed to stir the conscience of listeners during the penitential season of Lent, 1600.

Example 2 shows the Soul's answer to the temptations offered by 'Pleasure and Companions'.

La Rappresentatione di Anima e di Corpo
A recording of this is available on Naxos, 85540967.

Example 2 An extract from Cavalieri's *La Rappresentazione di anima e di Corpo* (1600)

The determination of the soul to resist these deceptive pleasures is expressed by musical repetitions that mirror the rhymes of the poetry and by the firm cadences with which these phrases end. Unlike the subtle rhythms of Peri's recitative this song is in marching $\frac{4}{4}$ time (the Oratorians thought of themselves as soldiers of Christ). The only touch of 'antique' modality is the F-major chord built on the flat 7th of the scale of G major in bars 4–5 and 6–7. It was this style of song that was to develop into the Italian aria and the English and French air of later baroque vocal music (such as the Ode discussed below).

Translation:
I do not believe you, no, no.
I know you are deceivers.
All those things that seem so delightful
At the end are all bitter.

Masque

A masque or mask was a kind of early 17th-century opera specially devised for important state occasions. Like contemporary Italian opera it combined vocal and instrumental music with dancing,

The Mask of Comus

lavish costumes and spectacular scenery. But, unlike Italian opera, spoken poetry was at least as important as song. The most famous English example is the *Mask of Comus* which was performed at Ludlow Castle in 1634 when the Earl of Bridgewater was installed as Lord President of Wales. The text is by England's most famous 17th-century poet, John Milton, the music by his friend, Henry Lawes. The poem is based on classical myths in which the sophisticated Comus (a personification of pleasure) attempts to seduce an innocent young lady (played by one of Bridgewater's children). Hers is the first song of the mask:

Example 3   The opening bars of an air by Henry Lawes in Milton's *Mask of Comus* (1634)

This is a prayer to Echo, a mythological nymph who 'lives unseen' because she wasted away after being rejected by Narcissus until only her voice remained. The 'airy shell' is the dome of the sky, Meander is a winding river in what is now Turkey and 'margent' is its margin or bank.

Like Italian opera composers Lawes tried to set his texts with what he called 'just note and accent'. By this he meant that the melodic accents should correspond with the natural accents of spoken English. A good example is the so-called 'Scotch snap' on the word 'Echo' which throws a 'just accent' on the first syllable while the longer note on the second syllable mirrors the effect of the comma in spoken English. Subtleties of this sort are captured by a variety of dotted rhythms that originated in France but soon became characteristic of English baroque music.

Ode

An **ode** is a piece of poetry set to ceremonial music for occasions such as a coronation, a birthday or a banquet. Odes are always full of praise. Henry Purcell (1659–1695), who composed several odes, was inspired by older English composers such as Henry Lawes. He was also influenced by the emotional and chromatic style of Italian and French composers shown in Example 1 (page 70), as well as their simple melodious, diatonic style shown in Example 2 (page 71). As a servant in the royal court one of Purcell's duties was to set odes to music. Between 1689 and 1694 Purcell set six odes for the birthdays of Queen Mary II. The last of them, *Come ye Sons of Art Away*, contains some of the composer's finest and most varied music. It is scored for what are relatively large resources by 17th-century standards, and it includes:

◆ solos for a soprano and a bass and a duet for countertenors

◆ a four-part chorus of sopranos, altos, tenors and basses

◆ two treble recorders and two oboes

Come ye Sons of Art

An ode can also be a piece of Greek or Latin poetry, or a Byzantine sacred song, but here too the text offers praise.

Come ye Sons of Art is available on Hyperion, KING2. The text is probably by Nahum Tate, poet laureate and librettist of Purcell's opera *Dido and Aeneas*.

A countertenor is an adult male singer with a range similar to that of an alto.

- ◆ two trumpets

- ◆ a string orchestra (up to 24 players was usual at the time)

- ◆ a **continuo** ensemble consisting of one or more bass instruments (such as a cello or bass viol, a double bass or contrabass viol, perhaps with one or more bassoons) and one or more harmony instruments (such as a harpsichord, chamber organ, lute or harp).

The majestic overture is in the late 17th-century Italian style with three sections:

- ◆ a solemn **homophonic** largo in D major (bars 1–10)

- ◆ a fast movement with much **imitation** and **antiphonal** exchanges between wind and strings starting in bar 32

- ◆ a wonderfully expressive adagio (bars 44–59) that is as chromatic and dissonant as any Italian slow movement of the age. It contrasts strongly with the festive D-major movements on either side.

The orchestral 'Symphony' that follows sounds like the last section of the overture, but it turns out to be the opening **ritornello** of the second movement. Its diatonic, D-major melody falls into the same seven four-bar phrases that Purcell uses for the alto solo, like this:

In a vocal composition a ritornello is an instrumental passage.

A (bars 1–4) oboes	A (bars 5–8) violins	B (bars 9–12) oboes	C (bars 12³–16) oboes	B (bars 17–20) violins	C (bars 20³–24) violins	C (bars 24³–28) oboes with violins
A (bars 29–32) 'Come, come, ye Sons of Art'	A (bars 33–36) 'Come, come, ye Sons of Art'	B (bars 37–40) 'Tune all your voices'	C (bars 43–44) 'to celebrate'	B (bars 45–48) 'Tune all your voices'	C (bars 43–52) 'to celebrate'	C (bars 523–56) 'to celebrate'

All of this is then repeated in bars 57–84. Purcell has composed a movement lasting 84 bars from just three four-bar phrases!

'Sound the trumpet' is a duet for two countertenors built on a two-bar **ground bass**. Note the way that Purcell makes his singers sound like trumpets in the fanfare motifs of bars 7–8.

This duet is in AQAA, page 68.

The fourth movement is a repeat of the second movement omitting the alto solo. It ends a block of four movements all in the tonic key of D major.

The next three movements are in minor keys, so providing a contrast; the first, 'Strike the viol', is in binary form (AB).

The key of D major returns with the last movement, which is a **rondo** in which a refrain (A) alternates with contrasting episodes (BC) to form the pattern ABACA.

Queen Mary II died in December 1694 and her funeral was held in bitterly cold weather on 5 March 1695. As her coffin was carried in procession through the streets to Westminster Abbey a trombone quartet played a slow march by Purcell, adapted from music he had written for a play some years earlier. For the service itself Purcell composed an anthem (*Thou knowest, Lord, the secrets of our hearts*), which was followed by a solemn canzona for trombones. Later that year Purcell himself died and the same music was performed at his own funeral in Westminster Abbey. Listen to the march and decide which features of the movement make it suitable

The March and Canzona, known as the *The Funeral Music for Queen Mary*, are in AQAA, page 71. The performance on that CD is played on trumpets, with timpani.

for use as funeral march. Then listen to the canzona and decide how it differs from the march. Which of these two movements has a homphonic texture and which has a polyphonic texture?

Anthem

An anthem is a piece of choral music with a religious (often Biblical) text. Handel wrote four anthems for the coronation of George II and Queen Caroline in Westminster Abbey on 11 October 1727. Bypassing committees of bishops and archbishops, the King himself commissioned them from Handel calling him 'the famous composer to the opera'. All of them reflect the pomp and circumstance of the event, none more so than the shortest and most famous – *Zadok the Priest* – which was sung during the anointing ceremony and which has been performed at every British coronation since. Celebration as well as solemnity were required at this point, so Handel composed for a choir dividing into seven parts accompanied by an orchestra of perhaps as many as 100 performers.

Handel divides the text from the Old Testament First Book of Kings into three sections. In the first section he reserves trumpets and drums for the first entry of the chorus singing the text 'Zadok the priest and Nathan the prophet anointed Solomon King' in massive seven-part homophony. This is perhaps the most exciting example of baroque terraced dynamics (sudden shifts from soft to loud and vice versa) and the vibrancy of the first tutti chord is further increased by the scoring, with the major 3rd (F$\sharp$) doubled in three octaves.

In the second section the rejoicing of the king's subjects is suggested by a triple-time dance with skipping dotted rhythms. The diatonic harmony consists, with only a couple of exceptions, of tonic and dominant chords. This allows full participation of the natural trumpets and drums.

In the third section the chordal setting of 'God save the King' contrasts with the **monophonic** setting of 'May the King live for ever' and the detached chords at the start of the Alleluia and Amen.

Zadok the Priest

Today people often use the term 'anthem' to mean 'a solemn song in which everyone joins' such as the 'National Anthem'. See 'pop anthems', page 80.

Zadok the Priest is in AQAA, page 73. The King's Consort has recorded a reconstruction of the 1727 coronation: *The Coronation of King George II* is a two CD-set available from Hyperion, CDA67286.

Note though that many performances and recordings get louder throughout the opening ritornello.

A natural trumpet is a trumpet without valves. Because of this it can play only a limited number of different pitches.

Test yourself

1. What is a ground bass?

    ....

    ....

2. Name **two** ways in which you think that *Zadok the Priest* was musically suitable for a coronation.

    ....

    ....

3. Name **two** differences between an ode and an anthem.

    ....

    ....

Overture

An overture is a piece of music written to come at the beginning of something. That something might be an opera, a play or a baroque dance suite – see page 57. In 1811 Beethoven was commissioned to write the music for a play called *The Ruins of Athens* which was to receive its first performance at the opening of a new theatre in Budapest. Although the music was successful at the opening of the theatre in 1812, the only item that is still regularly performed is the overture. Ten years later Beethoven learned that a revised version of *The Ruins of Athens* was to be produced at the opening of the new Josefstadt Theatre in Vienna. Obviously dissatisfied with the original overture Beethoven immediately set to work to write a new one called *The Consecration of the House*. It was premiered on 3 October 1822. By this stage Beethoven was profoundly deaf, but he insisted on directing the performance from the piano aided by a sub-conductor and the leader of the orchestra. Despite the inevitable problems the new overture was a success, and Beethoven – by now acknowledged throughout Europe as a towering genius – was called again and again to acknowledge the rapturous applause that he could see but not hear.

We know that Beethoven had unbounded admiration for Handel, but the clue to his use of baroque fugal style in this particular overture is contained in the title of the revised work. 'Consecration' normally means the act of making something sacred, and so is associated with solemn church services. But for Beethoven art, poetry, drama and especially music *were* sacred. Therefore just as a new church can be consecrated by a priest, so a new theatre – a temple of art – can be consecrated by music in an appropriate style. And the appropriate style for great solemnity was then, as it always had been, the style of a long-dead composer.

It is significant that Beethoven's title is a combination of French – *Ouverture*, and German – *Die Weihe des Hauses*. The baroque French overture began with a majestic slow section, usually in common time, and nearly always dotted rhythms (see page 85). The most famous example is the overture to Handel's *Messiah* (Example 4a).

Example 4

(a) Handel: Overture to *Messiah*, bars 1–4

(b) Beethoven: Overture to The Consecration of the House, bars 4–9

Equally common in the French overture are trills like those in bars 2 and 4 of Example 4a. These feature prominently in the climactic repeat of Beethoven's first theme (strings and bassoon in bar 31). Yet another characteristic of French overture style is a rapid scalic ascent to the first melody note. Called a *tirade*, it comes before each eight-bar phrase of Beethoven's melody (see the start of Example

The Consecration of the House

A recording of this work is available on Deutsche Grammophon, 427 2562.

We will discuss another overture by Beethoven on page 89.

4b) and adds terrific energy to the majestic theme. Finally notice the way three trombones – symbols of solemnity from earliest times – echo the cadences of these phrases (Example 4b, bars 7–8 plus bars 8–9, 20–21 and 24–25 in the score).

The second section of a baroque French overture was generally fugal in style. Many people think of fugue as musical rocket science, and they are not far wrong. Like ballistics, fugal composition requires quite a lot of brains. But just as ballistics can lead to one of the most exciting experiences of raw energy – the launch of a space rocket – so fugal composition can lead to an experience of raw musical energy. And that is what you can hear in the rest of Beethoven's overture.

Idyll

Siegfried Idyll

A recording of Wagner's *Siegfried Idyll* is available on Deutsche Grammophon, 4236132.

In 1864 the composer Richard Wagner fell in love with Cosima von Bülow, the strikingly beautiful daughter of Liszt and wife of the conductor Hans von Bülow. His love was reciprocated, so when, in 1865, Wagner was compelled to leave Germany and seek political asylum in Switzerland, Cosima followed him. Together they found a house called Triebschen on the shores of Lake Lucerne. Von Bülow raised no objections to their union because his own marriage had by this time become so unhappy that both he and Cosima had already contemplated divorce. In 1868 Wagner began work on the last act of *Siegfried*, an opera about a young hero who braves the wrath of the gods and awakens the heroine from her long sleep. On 6 June 1868 Cosima gave birth to Wagner's only son. His name (did you guess?) was Siegfried.

Living in wedded bliss in his idyllic house, Wagner began work on a single-movement composition for a large chamber ensemble consisting of five woodwinds, three brass instruments and a string quintet. The melodic material came from the last act of *Siegfried*, but it was combined and developed in a form that Wagner called an idyll. Wagner borrowed the term from literature. An idyll is a type of verse or prose that describes a peaceful pastoral scene. He organised secret rehearsals of the *Siegfried Idyll* and on Christmas Day 1870 the 13-member ensemble gathered on the staircase at Wagner's home to surprise Cosima with what Wagner described as 'a symphonic birthday greeting'.

Example 5

(a) bars 29–33
Molto tranquillo

(b) bars 37–38

Example 5a shows part of the first theme of the idyll. It includes three motifs that you can hear in various transformations throughout the piece. The first (x) is part of an ascending scale with a characteristic triplet rhythm. It is immediately repeated in the cello part, then is varied by the addition of a discordant note (C♯ in x^1) and by being turned upside down (x^2). Motif y is a falling five-note motif forming the intervals of a tone, a minor 3rd and two more tones. Can you see that the flute motif (Example 5b) is the same motif transposed up two octaves and a 5th with a new dotted rhythm? Finally motif z is a falling 7th that crops up again in bars 39–40.

When Wagner called the idyll 'symphonic' he did not mean that it was a symphony, nor that it should be performed by a symphony orchestra (though it often is nowadays). He meant that the themes and their developments are to be enjoyed in purely musical terms. This is important because it is quite possible to find the origin of every motif in the last act of *Siegfried*. Example 6a, for instance, shows the motif in the horn part of bars 259–263.

Example 6   Wagner, extracts from the *Siegfried Idyll* (1870) and the last act of *Siegfried* (1871)

This horn melody is an example of a **leitmotif**. You don't need to know what part of the opera it is taken from to hear that it expresses joy: it is fast, in the major, diatonic, and leaps joyfully up and down. Now listen to the clarinet motif heard in bars 262–263. It too comes from the opera but what matters is that, together with the piping oboe motif (Example 6b), it is meant to represent birdsong.

We previously encountered leitmotifs on page 43.

Remember: an idyll describes a pastoral scene.

Another theme to look out for is a traditional cradle-song first heard in the oboe part of bars 91–101 (Example 6c):

Example 6c
(c) bars 91–101

As with so many romantic compositions the form does not correspond with any conventional structures of earlier periods. However there is a beginning, a middle and an end, partly determined by keys and partly by Wagner's use of the motifs we have discussed.

Test yourself

1. Name **two** ways in which Wagner suggests the pastoral aspect of an 'idyll' in the *Siegfried Idyll*?

   ....
   ....
   ....
   ....

2. Name **two** musical ways in which you think that *Consecration of the House* was appropriate for the opening of a new theatre.

   ....
   ....
   ....
   ....

3. In what **two** musical ways does the *Siegfried Idyll* reflect the occasion for which it was written?

   ....
   ....
   ....
   ....

Fanfares

Fanfare for the Common Man

Fanfare for the Common Man is available on Naxos, 8550282.

Progressive-rock musicians Emerson, Lake and Palmer released a rock version of *Fanfare for the Common Man*. You can hear this on their album *Fanfare for the Common Man*, Castle Music (CMEDD110) or the album *Live at the Albert Hall*, Castle Music (CMRCD228).

Fanfares are ceremonial brass music. Their traditional purpose was to announce something such as the arrival of a monarch, so they are often short and dramatic. In the middle of the second world war the English conductor Eugene Goosens asked the American composer Aaron Copland for a patriotic fanfare for the Cincinnati Symphony Orchestra. Copland's work was an immediate success when it was premiered in Cincinnati in the USA on 12 March 1943 and has since become the most famous fanfare of the 20th century. The composer says in his autobiography that 'the challenge was to compose a traditional fanfare, direct and powerful, yet with a contemporary sound'.

Copland writes for the instruments traditionally associated with a fanfare, but the forces are larger than one would expect:

◆ four horns in F

◆ three trumpets in B♭

◆ three trombones and a tuba

◆ four timpani (tuned to F, B♭, d and f – the pitches of the tonic triad of B♭ major)

A tam-tam is a type of gong.

◆ bass drum and tam-tam.

In the introduction for percussion – itself something of a novelty – the two timpani notes are the tonic and dominant of B♭ major, the primary key of the piece. The strong–weak, on-beat quaver rhythm (a type of Scotch snap) punctuates the brass music of the first 40 bars.

There are five melodic ideas, each of them identified by a capital letter in Example 7.

Example 7

(a) bars 13–21

(b) bars 28–32

When you listen to bars 6–12 can you hear how Copland's theme ends its second phrase with a 'wrong note'? It begins with an arpeggio of E♭, but ends with F which does not belong to the triad of E♭. The use of primary triads with extra notes certainly produces that 'contemporary sound' Copland sought. He also adds to the contemporary feel by augmenting the rhythms (see bar 21, where the semiquavers of bar 11 have been doubled in length to produce quavers) and using more than one time signature.

The texture is entirely homorhythmic, the two parts having exactly the same rhythms as they move together, mostly forming consonant intervals of the 4th, 5th and 6th. Intense discords such as the two chords marked by asterisks in example 7b, which are formed by passing notes between the chords of G minor and C minor 7, stand out and introduce a modal flavour to the piece.

The music of the next phase is homophonic and diatonic, using only the pitches of a scale of B♭ major, up to the first chord of bar 30 (Example 7b). But the first 7th chord introduces an A♭. This is the flattened 7th degree of B♭ major, and it intensifies the modal flavour of Copland's harmony.

Copland also makes use of the characteristics of his instruments to produce particular effects. Copland moves from chord V of B♭ major to the very bright chord of D major with which the fanfare unexpectedly ends with an enormous crescendo (see *right*). The dazzling brilliance of this conclusion is intensified by the omission of the tuba and by scoring the chord so that all the other instruments are playing in their highest registers.

The *Fanfares Across the Thames* by British composer Jonathan Dove (b. 1959) were commissioned by the London Millennium Bridge Trust for the opening of London's Millennium Bridge on 9 May 2000, when they were performed by students from the Guildhall School of Music and Drama. The pedestrian bridge links

Can you also see this happen in Example 7 at the end of phrase B?

(e) triads a 3rd apart with A♮ common to all

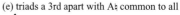

The first of the *Fanfares Across the Thames* is in AQAA, page 116. Milton Babbit's *Fanfare for All* is in AQAA, page 107.

the City of London and St Paul's Cathedral with the Tate Modern and Globe Theatre in Southwark. In the first fanfare two brass bands (with percussion) played in antiphony on opposite banks of the Thames, joining together only in the final four bars. After the Queen and Bishop of London had opened the bridge, a second fanfare was performed. In this, the two brass bands were joined by a wind band playing on a barge in mid-river. Thus the music symbolises the purpose of the bridge – to link the two communities on either side of the Thames.

The *Fanfare for All* was written by the American composer Milton Babbitt (b. 1916) for the Meridian Arts Ensemble in 1993.

Listen to both of these works and then list the features that identify them as fanfares.

Music at Princess Diana's funeral

Song for Athene

This is in AQAA, page 110.

The English composer John Tavener (b. 1944) wrote *Song for Athene* in 1993. Composed for unaccompanied choir it was written in memory of Athene Hariades, the daughter of a close friend who tragically died that year. The words are taken from Shakespeare's *Hamlet* and the Christian Orthodox funeral service. The work was chosen as the moving conclusion for the funeral service of Diana Princess of Wales in 1997.

Candle in the Wind

The 1973 version, celebrating the life of film star Marilyn Monroe, is on a number of compilations including *A Perfect Love II* (Global RADCD 105). The 1997 version is available on Mercury PTCD 1 568 109-2.

Elton John's *Funeral for a Friend* is in AQAA, page 104.

The original version of Elton John's *Candle in the Wind* was released in 1973. He rewrote the words for the song's performance at Pincess Diana's funeral. Some of the key words and phrases in both versions of the song remain the same: it is in a major key and in $\frac{4}{4}$ metre. Important musical differences between the two versions are:

✦ the later version is higher in pitch than the 1973 recording

✦ bass guitar, lead guitar and percussion are used in the 1973 version but not in the later one

✦ the vocal chorus effects used in 1973 are more complex than those used in 1997.

Pop anthems

Do They Know it's Christmas?

Artists who performed included Status Quo, Led Zeppelin, The Who, David Bowie and Mick Jagger.

In 1985, Bob Geldof (of the Boomtown Rats) organised a live concert to be put on simultaneously in the USA and Britain using video links. Live Aid was one of the most important events in popular music history: not only were many of the world's top pop stars performing at the same event, but all proceeds went to famine victims in Africa.

Live Aid was inspired by the success of Band Aid's single *Do They Know it's Christmas?* which was released in November 1984. Co-written by Geldof and Ultravox's Midge Ure, the song was composed and performed for the purpose of raising money for famine relief. It became the best-selling UK single of the 1980s and some of the most well-known pop musicians of the time, including Wham, Sting, Spandau Ballet, Bananarama and Duran Duran, performed on it.

The song opens with a four-bar introduction that features tubular bells. The instrumental and vocal textures vary throughout this song – each verse has a slightly different feel to it and the song builds up gradually until the climatic 'Feed the World' chorus at the end. The upbeat tempo, major key, tubular bells, and solo and chorus voices made the song catchy and popular, yet the hard-hitting lyrics remind us why the song was composed. The structure is as follows:

Intro	Verse 1	Verse 2	Verse 3	Bridge	End chorus (fades to end)
Four-bar introduction with tubular bells chiming at the start of each bar.	No accompaniment except for a heavy bass line punctuated with deep drum beats. Solo voice.	Tempo changes and becomes more upbeat and lively. Solo voice and then duet.	Whole cast of musicians singing together in harmony. Tubular bells chime on the first beat of each bar.	Link section in the minor key followed by an instrumental interlude.	Whole cast of musicians singing 'Feed the World' in harmony.

Three Lions on a Shirt was composed by Ian Broudie of the Lightning Seeds with lyrics by David Baddiel and Frank Skinner. The song's theme is the performance of England's football team and it was released during the run-up to the 1998 World Cup. The song is in a major key and in $\frac{4}{4}$ metre and includes sections sung by a football crowd.

In December 1976 Bob Marley and the Wailers agreed to play at a peace concert in Kingston, Jamaica, in an attempt to bring together opposing political parties. There had been much violence between members of the two parties during the previous months.

Although Marley was himself shot and wounded shortly before, he went ahead with the concert. The performance featured *One Love*, a Rastafarian (see page 102) song in a major key and in $\frac{4}{4}$ metre. The theme of this song is love and unity, and its lyrics were particularly relevant to the situation in Jamaica at the time. 'One love, one heart', sang Marley, 'Let's get together an' feel all right'. He brought Michael Manley and Edward Seaga, the two party leaders, on stage and lifted their joined hands into the air in a symbol of reconciliation.

Three Lions on a Shirt

The song is available (track 16) on *Like you do…Best of the Lightning Seeds*, Sony, 1997 (Sony 01-4890342-10). It contrasts strongly with the archetypal football anthem from 1970, *Back Home*: do these two songs have any features in common?

One Love

One Love is available (track 12) on *One love: The very best of Bob Marley and the Wailers*, a compilation released by Tuff Gong in 2001 (Tuff Gong/Island 548 853-2).

Test yourself

1. In *One Love*:

    (a) Are the chords used on-beat or off-beat? ....

    (b) Name two percussion instruments that you can hear.

    ....

    (c) Which of the following occurs in the chorus?

    call and response   homophony   polyphony

    (d) What sort of pattern does the bass guitar provide?

    ....

2. In *Three Lions on a Shirt*

    (a) Circle the melodic interval in the two-note riff sung by the football crowd.

    major 3rd   minor 3rd   major 6th   minor 6th   minor 2nd

    (b) When the chorus enter do they sing in unison or harmony?

    ....

Did you notice that the upper note was slightly sharp?

(c) When the bass-guitar line enters, the bass line moves mostly in descending steps of which scale?

chromatic   modal   diatonic   whole tone

Composing

A fanfare

Compose a fanfare for a special event. Remember that a fanfare is intended to be a strident call to attention but often has a quieter section in the middle. They are usually composed for brass (although any loud and bright-sounding instrument like a saxophone or a suitable keyboard timbre will do) and the use of percussion is quite common. If you are writing a fanfare remember that it is not an excuse for endless arpeggios and scales. Listen again to *Fanfare for the Common Man* to give you some ideas.

A team song

Compose a song for a school sports team. Team songs are usually written to a formula. Although promoted as pop songs with the team singing along with a group they are usually marches with a verse and chorus.

A march or music for a procession

If you want to compose a march or music for a procession, listen to some marches (by Sousa, Eric Coates, Walton or Elgar). The first feature to get right is pace. Imagine soldiers marching, or people in a procession or a bride walking up the aisle. How fast should the footsteps be? Next think about melody. Many marches include an uplifting and often singable tune in a slower middle section (which is often repeated in a very grand version at the end). Listen to the march melody in Elgar's *Pomp and Circumstance* March No. 1 – better known as *Land of Hope and Glory* – which builds to a climax on the highest note and that of Pomp and Circumstance No. 4, all of whose phrases finish with an optimistic rising interval. Not all processions are formal marches, however. In recent years politicians have sometimes entered to pop music at their party conferences. Boxers also like to make a grand entry and parade around the ring. Remember too, that there is a place for solemn music. A quiet and thoughtful instrumental interlude can be just as telling as a rousing fanfare or march.

School occasions

Compose a piece of music to be played at the last assembly before the Christmas break. It should be for two trumpets and trombone. The players are of a reasonable standard. Your piece should last about one minute and be in a celebratory style. Make use of at least one familiar Christmas melody and open and close the movement with some fanfare-like passages. Write your score with the trumpets at sounding pitch. However for performance of the piece you will need to provide trumpet parts in B♭. This means transposing the parts up a tone (for example if the tonic note of your movement is C then the trumpets will need to have parts with a tonic note of D).

Compose a movement to be played during a visit by students to a local residential home for senior citizens. It should be for two flutes and piano and should last for no more than two minutes. The two flautists are of a good technical standard, the pianist less so. The performers have several lively pieces to play and would like you to